RICHES TO RAGS
(and back again)
I've Got A Song For That

EVIE THOMPSON
(EVIE T.)

RICHES TO RAGS
(AND BACK AGAIN)
I'VE GOT A SONG
FOR THAT

2006

RICHES TO RAGS
(and back again)
I've Got A Song For That

TABLE OF CONTENTS

ACKNOWLEDGEMENTS

I was blessed with much support from angels while writing this book—both in human form and more ethereal forms.

I would especially like to thank my therapist, Jane Morris, for leading me out of the darkness and into the light of my true self. She is my mentor, my mother, and my friend. I don't think I would have made it through without her, and I wouldn't have wanted to try.

Many thanks, also, to my soul sisters from my women's group (Pam Smithson, Mary Drake, Leita Spoto, Cynthia Robertson, Roz Laizure, Claudia Martin, Auralee Smith, Elizabeth Raley, Joette Trieber, and Carolyn Homan). They provided the manger from which I could resurrect myself from the carnage of my past.

I would really like to thank my children for putting up with me as I was while they were young. I know it wasn't easy. I did my best, but I am aware that, very often, my best may not have been good enough. I hope they know that I always loved them no matter how it may have appeared.

I am grateful to all my deceased loved ones (and maybe not-so-loved ones). I know you're there, and I know you did your best while you were in your bodies, given your circumstances. I know it isn't easy down here. May we all be forgiven.

Thank you to Roz Laizure for editing my precious manuscript with an open heart and a scrupulous mind, and letting me drive her crazy in the process.

Many, many, many thanks to David Vasquez from Moonlight Studios in Los Angeles. He was involved in the recording of all but three of the 44 songs in this book. His talent is amazing and working with him has been one of my greatest joys.

And, last but not least, thank you to all the Beings of Light who were appointed to watch over and guide me through this lifetime. I must be quite a challenging appointment!

PREFACE

How do you follow an empire? Most people don't ask themselves that question before they go on to build one. And they probably don't consider what the effects will be on successive generations. I have spent the last 57 years trying to figure that out. One thing you don't do if you're a member of an empire is to point out that the emperor has no clothes on. You don't talk about it, in or out of the family, and you certainly don't put it in print lest it finds its way into the hands of a publisher.

Even as I begin to write this, I can feel the pressure of the empire crushing me. When I got the brilliant idea to write a book about my family and my life, I was immediately besieged by a variety of physical symptoms (trouble breathing, pains in my body, and I ended up in the hospital for one night with "food poisoning"—all signals from the emperors and empresses (most of them dead by now, but no less influential) that I had better shut up. Now that I think about it, "shut up" was by far the most consistent and ingrained message I was given while growing up. It's in my cells and imprinted on my soul and it is very difficult to get beyond it. My brother, Bobby (Robert), calls the voices from the not-so-distant past "the committee", and while it may be amusing at first listen, the voices are vociferous and they are vicious. Their intention is now, as it was then, to keep the underlings in their place and keep the family secrets under wraps.

A number of books have been written about my family (my mother's side, at least), and my siblings are much better with the facts, names, and dates than I am. So I will not focus so much on names, dates, historical data, or chronology, but rather about my experience of being in my family and about how it felt to me, because there is always more than one side to a story, and I can only tell mine. My siblings might have a different perspective, but, again, I can only tell my story from mine. Maybe I'm the only one who will ever hear it, but it is important to tell. Most of the players have passed away by now, which is also very sad and is also part of the story.

I spent a good portion of my life being a musician/singer/songwriter. I am including CDs with this book, as each song is an encapsulated version of what was going on in my life or the world around me at the time. I will reference each song during the telling of the story.

I now see that the microcosm of my life is part of the larger drama of the macrocosm. My own little empire was actually part of a huge, immovable, megalithic monster, otherwise known as the "patriarchal system", which systematically sets about to murder souls and is its own form of ethnic cleansing. My mother, bless her soul, was one of the victims of this system. I think she is probably the only one of my ancestors who would appreciate my attempts to set the record straight and tell the truth (at least my truth) about it all. My siblings and I have suffered greatly as well. This is for them as much as for me.

A few months ago, my niece, Adelaide, after having witnessed a scene between my brother, sister, and I that was particularly painful, asked me, "What happened to all of you?" I felt the pain in her voice, for she has suffered as well, and my answer is in the writing of this book. Perhaps it will finally silence the "committee", and the "Field Family Curse" will have been lifted from future generations.

Hopefully, the EMPIRE WON'T STRIKE BACK! (On the other hand, maybe my family will pay me to not publish this!)

Evie Thompson
Nevada City, California
(Labor Day, 2005)

AT-ON(E)CE

What first
appears
to be
a void
is really
shadows
of myself
a dark
and murky
underworld
that spews up
demons
one by one
til truth
is known
and every piece
put into place
to make the whole
light up
at-on(e)ce

Evie Thompson, 1981

CHAPTER ONE
Eve Gets the Boot
(The Early Years)

Song #1—*Lady of the Stars*

I have a memory of another time and place—perhaps before I came into this body—where there was perfect peace—where I was totally surrounded and enveloped by a boundless love—where nothing was needed and all was given. Rather like the Garden of Eden, and then...

I don't know how to explain this, but I was conscious from the moment I came out of my mother's womb that I had been dropped off on a barbaric planet. Not only that, but I was definitely delivered to the wrong family. I must have had some heavy karma. Beam me up, Scottie. ET, phone home...

I was born Evelyn Marshall Boggs on March 1, 1948, in New York City. My father called me "Teensy" and my older sister, Barbara, called me "Twinkletoes" ("Twinks", for short). So from all the diminutive nicknames, I gather I was rather small compared to all those who seemed to tower over me. My mother came from what was at the time a very wealthy, famous family (Marshall Field—the store in Chicago of the same name), etc. My father was an ex-navy officer, neurosurgeon, and accomplished a long list of other impressive things. Sounds good so far, doesn't it? Not!

We lived in a very large house, at the end of a very long road, in the midst of a very long list of pedigreed names in Manhasset, Long Island. Most people would probably kill to live in a house like that, but it scared the hell out of me. I had to run full-tilt to get from my room at one end of the house to my mother's room at the other. In between, I had to pass my brother's room (good for some torture), my sisters' rooms (fairly neutral territory), and the dreaded guest room that was, according to my brother, filled with ghosts and monsters. Not a trip I wanted to make frequently. In more ways than just our geographical location, I was inconsolably lonely and isolated.

One rather humorous, though painful, incident at this house stands out in my memory. I was just about to walk down the very steep (uncarpeted) back staircase when my feet went out from under me. I bounced down every step of that staircase on my tailbone. The amusing part was that every time I hit a step, I farted. My sister, Sally, was at the bottom of the staircase, and by the time I arrived on the last step, she was doubled over laughing. At the time, I didn't find it funny at all, but I can appreciate how Sally might have thought so. I was to repeat that performance two more times in my older years, both times on icy, outside steps. My tailbone is still jammed and has arthritis. This was just the beginning of endless blows to this poor little body.

I was, by all accounts, a bit of a brat, or so they told me. I guess I threw a lot of tantrums (no one thought to ask why). I was the fourth and last child and apparently not a welcome addition, or so it felt to me at the time. My chief impression of my younger years was of being left alone quite a bit of the time and receiving very little in the way of nurturing, comfort, or physical affection. My mother was sick most of the time and started spending more and more time in the hospital, and later on, in mental institutions. We were left in the hands of some pretty brutal governesses, or my father, and I'm not sure which was worse.

Some of my earliest memories (I'm not sure of the chronological order): someone trying to smother me with a pillow; being thrown against a wall; one governess rubbing my own feces in my face when I went to the bathroom in my toy chest in the middle of the night because I was too scared to get up and go to the bathroom in the dark; another governess putting her hand over my nose and mouth to shut me up until I passed out; being molested with and without my sister, Sally, (usually in the bathtub) by my alcoholic, neurosurgeon father; being spanked with a hair brush; being spanked with a wire hanger. Later on in life, I wrote this poem:

Don't grieve
little girl
you got stuck
upside down
in your bed
your mother's
gone off
to the nuthouse
your parakeet's sick
there's a ghost
in your closet
the nurse tried
to smother
your cries
but don't grieve
little girl

it will pass.

One thing I learned at a very young age was not to let anyone see my feelings. I was told that anything I did would make my mother sick or send her back to the hospital again, i.e., I was responsible for her life and death. I learned to shut myself off and shut myself up and pretend nothing was wrong, so I would protect her. I was afraid all the time. I lived in fear that anything that I said or did to call attention to what was going on would be disastrous to the delicate balance of my family dynamics and most especially to the physical and mental health of my mother. I never knew when the next disaster, alcoholic mood, mental breakdown or bodily invasion would happen, so I became hypervigilant and could never let down my guard. I feared for my own life and the lives of my brothers and sisters. And there was absolutely no one I could turn to or trust. FEAR was my prevailing state of mind.

Song #2—*Secrets and Lies*

Another lesson learned very early on was that there was very little use for females, and that included my poor brother who happened to be the son of a female (who isn't?). My grandfather, Marshall Field III, still believed in a patriarchal system. So when he died, my mother inherited a pittance, comparatively speaking, and her children (myself included) inherited $350,000 apiece (which is nothing to sneeze at except my male cousins, who were the exact same relationship to my grandfather, inherited somewhere in the neighborhood of $300 million each). This was very painful for my mother and all of us, not so much in terms of the actual money issue but in terms of the message it sent, received loud and clear: You don't count, you don't matter. You're a woman, or the son of a woman, and are therefore insignificant.

One of the unfortunate side effects of that particular policy was to create generations of very angry women who felt powerless, worthless, and ended up having difficulties with men, and because of some very unfortunate role models, couldn't live with 'em and couldn't live without 'em. It also created the syndrome of marrying men who married us for money that, in reality, we did not have, but try telling that to someone who is blinded by the illusion of fame and fortune.

At any rate, as a result of this particular aspect of my upbringing, I had absolutely no self-esteem or sense of self-worth. I hated my body, was filled with self-loathing, and wished I had been born a man.

Song #3—*What if Every Little Girl*

On the upside, we took many great trips, and I think we actually might have had some fun during those times, although the negativity far outweighed the relief of the trips. We spent a number of springs in Boca Grande, Florida or in the Bahamas. Summers during my early years were spent in Martha's Vineyard. One summer we went across the country with all four kids (that, in itself, might have driven my mother over the edge).

I actually enjoyed visiting my grandfather's estate in Lloyd's Neck, Long Island. It was a surreal existence and a far cry from my current life experience. He had approximately 80 servants of one sort or another, including one person to squeeze the toothpaste. The mansion was so big, I never did figure out where everything was. There was an indoor pool, tennis courts, boat house, yacht, stables that were nicer than most people's houses, and my favorite, little electric cars for us to drive around the estate. Curiously, I have no bad memories of my grandfather. He was always very kind to me, a little distant, but decent. I was around 8 years old when he died, I think, so I had very little time with him. But I have had many years of carrying his unfortunate financial legacy around my neck like an albatross.

His wife, Evie (aka Bunny), after whom I was named, was rather like our version of the Wicked Witch of the West, only worse. I'm not sure what happened to her to make her turn out the way she did, but she, too, was an alcoholic and meaner than a hornet. Some called her Poison Evie, and she certainly had a devastating effect of her own on my mother, uncle, and aunt. She disowned me the first time because I was "living in sin" with my second husband-to-be, but I was reinstated when we got married. Ultimately, she disowned me and cut me out of her will when I stood up to her about treating my mother badly. I'm sure I wasn't as diplomatic as I might be now, but that was just the way she was—"cut off their heads." You did not 'piss her off' without severe repercussions.

I do remember some good times with her as well, though, and was very sad when she cut me off because she literally never talked to me again, even when we were in the same room.

I had my first cigarette when I was 8 years old and my first drink (other than just wine) at the age of 9. I drank, alcoholically, from the age of 12 and was already having blackouts. One year in Martha's Vineyard, my sister, Sally, and I (age 12) were driving in a car with some of my brother's friends, going 120 miles an hour on a back road, and hit a patch of sand. The car flipped a bunch of times and when it was all over, Sally's head was cracked open. I thought she was dead because there was green stuff all over the place (her brains, I thought), but it turned out it was crème de menthe. We were all very drunk. Sally had the most obvious injuries, and to this day, I have cracked ribs and spinal problems which are very painful and getting more so as I get older. She was evacuated to a hospital in Boston and almost died.

The following summer, or maybe it was the previous summer, Sally broke her collarbone on the trampoline and was confined to her bed. She was bored, so she started throwing my crayons out of the window. Without thinking, I climbed out on the roof to retrieve them and fell off the roof onto a brick walkway. I shattered my foot and ankle, broke all the bones in my toes, and had a banjo cast on my foot, with pins thru the toes and elastic bands pulling them up for six months.

These two incidents were very early examples of a growing, unconscious urge for self-destruction. Around the same time as all these physical accidents were happening, we were being molested by my father and God knows whom else. There was some talk of some of my brother's friends getting in on the action, although I have no conscious memory of that, which is probably a blessing.

We were drinking ourselves into oblivion and my mother was taking every prescription drug known to mankind.

Song #4—*Mother, Where Were You?*

Somewhere in between the car accident and falling off the roof, my parents got a divorce and my father left. My first reaction was great relief to get him out of the house and away from me, soon followed by a terrible feeling of abandonment. This curious ambivalence was to set the trend for all of my relationships with men in my later life. I'd get into a relationship or marriage and then (usually 1½ to 2 years later)

I'd be desperate to get out. I'd bolt, then feel overwhelming pain about being abandoned.

We were never allowed to really be children. It seems to me we were expected to spring fully formed from the womb with no imperfections. Toilet training was a battle; eating was a battle; noise was a no-no; squirming, wiggling, and other kid things were frowned upon. Don't cry. Don't laugh too loud. Don't scream. Don't sing unless you do it properly. Don't stomp your feet. Don't talk back. Don't need anything. Don't put your elbows on the table. Don't make a mess. Don't breathe. Don't feel. Don't make a mistake. Don't, don't, don't, don't...most of all, don't tell your mother anything.

I often wonder if the "DON'T" thing wasn't a hand-me-down aspect of the Victorian era—a trait coming from being of British aristocratic descent. For me it was stifling, rigid, and destroyed any kind of natural exuberance and energy a normal little kid would have. My brother's nickname for me was "Evil—a seemingly benign, childish epithet. But given the above, and all the other circumstances in my life, it contributed to my belief that there was something really bad and wrong with me, and I had better keep myself under wraps and exert an enormous amount of self-control to make sure I didn't infect anyone else with my presence.

Song #5—W.A.S.P. Blues

I think most of us on our side of the family grew up with the expectation that in order for us to be acceptable we had to follow in the family's footsteps, i.e., if we weren't bankers, publishers, corporate magnates, hot-shot lawyers, diplomats, or something along those lines, our lives were meaningless. Unfortunately, my mother and all of her children were not gifted in those areas. We all ended up being writers, musicians, and bohemian-types that were not highly regarded in the family system. It was mildly tolerated to be those things provided, of course, you were famous and started another empire. God forbid you should do it because you loved it and couldn't not do it.

I bring this topic up now because in childhood usually you can see the seeds of unique and individual gifts that will become the adult's contribution to the world. We were so repressed, oppressed, suppressed and controlled, our innate creative processes and hidden talents had no chance of finding their own course and future destiny. Instead of support, we were slapped down. Instead of encouragement, we received discouragement. Instead of family as cheer-leading section, ours was family as competitors and critics. Even though we were given access to all that money and privilege could buy (in terms of piano lessons, riding lessons, skating lessons, dance lessons, tennis lessons, opera, musicals, etc.), it wasn't for the expression of the soul—it was more for adornment and enhancement of the Field family cultural image.

Song #6—*A Little Child Shall Lead Us*

My mother had a peculiar habit of setting us up to compete with her (piano, tennis, backgammon, croquet, etc.) and then being really upset if we beat or surpassed her. So great was her need to win, she actually cheated with us and even while playing with her little grandchildren. We were forced into the competition, but then very subtly (or not so subtly) programmed to let her come out the winner. This proved to be unfortunate programming for all of us in our future endeavors, as most of us stopped short of all that we could have been or done (although it's never too late!). If you throw this strangeness in with the mix of thinking we were responsible for her life or death—well, you get the picture...succeed and we kill our mother. None of us wanted to be murderers, so we killed off parts of ourselves instead.

Nothing else springs to mind from my early years, and I'm having an image of myself in my teenage years (my "ugly" years) so I'll follow that train of thought to the next chapter.

CHAPTER TWO
The Ugly Duckling
(The Teenage Years)

By the time I reached my teenage years, I was deeply and profoundly miserable. I wanted to be anyone but who I was and anywhere but where I was. I had been led to believe (not sure where it came from) that I was stupid (one of my father's favorite words), ugly, and fat. In fact, I was very good in school, wasn't in the least bit ugly, and was just starting to put on some extra weight—the beginning of my insides not matching my outsides.

I'm going to insert two songs here that I wrote in my 50's, from an adult point of view, to begin the healing of my "inner child."

Song #7—*God Don't Make No Junk*
Song #8—*If I'm Good Enough for God*

I didn't know quite what to make about my burgeoning breasts and raging hormones, and there was little to no guidance through this period of my life. My mother remarried when I was about 12 years old, and she was in, more than out, of mental and medical hospitals. When she was at home, she was pretty much out of it most of the time and couldn't quite keep it together enough to raise her children properly. I was still carrying around an enormous amount of pain from the early years but was unable to tell anyone about it. So I suffered, in silence, and did just about anything to drown out my inner chaos, including drinking alcohol, smoking, bingeing and purging, and becoming sexually active far too young for my own good.

My new stepfather, Peter, was definitely a step up (no pun intended) from my biological father. He was very kind to me and I adored him right from the beginning. He was also an alcoholic—no surprise there. My first memory of him was when he came to visit my mother, forgot to put his emergency brake on, and his car rolled down the hill of our driveway and landed in the bushes. One of my last memories of him, many years later, was when he was walking through the living room with his hands behind his back, looking up at the ceiling, failed to notice my mother doing exercises on the floor, stepped on her face and broke her nose and glasses. (I thought it was hysterical; she did not). These two memories pretty much sum up his personality—absent-minded professor; loveable, but off in the clouds somewhere. He was a glider pilot during WWII, and I don't think he ever came back to earth.

For some odd reason, I thought it would be a good idea to go to boarding school—anything to get away from home. I don't know what I was thinking. I ended up going to The Masters School in Dobbs Ferry, New York (also known as Dobbs). I didn't do any better there than I did at home. Being with all girls was very strange. It was here I learned to stuff my face and then stick my finger down my throat so I didn't gain weight. I somehow managed to get a hold of cigarettes and alcohol even though they were not allowed (I was not alone in this!).

Two scenes stick out in my mind from my Dobbs' phase. One was the day that JFK was shot. I was playing field hockey and was devastated by the news, although I wasn't much interested in politics at the time. The other was a time when, before returning to school after a break, I drank a bottle of rum. Our chauffeur, Bill, had to drive back to school with me passed out in the back seat. This was one of my first blackouts, so I don't remember much except that he had to lie to the housemother and say I had a terrible case of the flu. I woke up a couple of days later in the infirmary and fell in love with the Beatles (playing on the radio when I awoke)...my love affair with music was being born, although I was generally too out of it to do anything constructive with it.

Then I had the brilliant idea I should do a year abroad. I ended up going to the Montesano School in Gstaad, Switzerland. I hated being cold and couldn't stand skiing at the time, so it wasn't a great success. We had to speak French most of the time. As a consequence, the other girls and I used to hide in the bathroom, smoke out the window, and talk in English (ever the rebel). I managed to get bronchial pneumonia, and my mother brought me back in a couple of months before the year was up and put me in The Hewitt's School (formerly Miss Hewitt's) as a day student, so I could live at home with her in our New York City apartment.

By this time, Mummy was in and out of hospitals and mental institutions more frequently, and I was drinking terpin hydrate (codeine) to get high at school. I also kept a bottle of Tanqueray gin in my desk so I could have a little nip to help me with my homework. My sister, Sally, got kicked out of yet another school in France, so she was home as well. I was dating an older man (not sure how much older) who I had no business dating, but that didn't stop me. I dumped him and then started dating another older man (a friend of my brother's) who was about ten years older than I. In a drunken fog, I lost my virginity at age 16 and was convinced I was in love with him. He called it off—I went berserk and swallowed a bottle of aspirin (thinking that would put me out of my misery). Thus began my first experience with therapy.

<u>Song #9—*Ticket Outta Here*</u>

Somewhere in the midst of all that chaos, I did manage to get quite proficient at the piano and started writing music. I wrote the school song for Hewitt's and also composed the music for a take-off on Hamlet (called *Shamlet*)—a show that one of my friends and I put on for the whole school. I wasn't prepared for how nervous I was while performing the show, so I took that as a sign I was not particularly gifted. I don't remember receiving a whole lot of support, for my blossoming talents, from my family, and there was really no one to talk me through the rather natural process of overcoming stage fright.

We spent a few summers during my teens at a ranch in Wyoming with my stepfather's four daughters. As you can imagine, there were frequent catfights and much sibling rivalry. How my mother managed six WILD teenage girls is beyond me. Come to think of it, she had one of her biggest nervous breakdowns on the ranch, so perhaps she didn't handle it at all. I fell in love (as did we all) with every working dude on the ranch and spent nights drinking with the boys in the bullpen (aptly named boys' quarters). One of the favorite pastimes was to hold a match or lighter in front of a can of deodorant or hairspray and incinerate bugs and bats. I went on a ten-day pack trip through the Tetons on horseback—a trip I would kill for now but I was too consumed with the boys I had left behind to appreciate it. However, thus began my love of the West.

During these years, my father remarried a woman who had even more money than my mother. She was also my best friend's mother. Add two more stepsisters and one stepbrother to the mix. It didn't help that my stepsister, Jay, was absolutely gorgeous, extremely popular with the boys, had a perfect hourglass figure, and didn't smoke or drink. She was due to inherit millions of dollars on her 18th and 21st birthdays. She could get and keep a tan (I, by contrast, was white, white, white). Her virginity outlasted mine by about fifteen years. Not only that, she was a sweetheart...damn. No envy there. I used all these facts to further lower myself in my own esteem.

Jay and I were allowed to go on a trip alone to Europe. All I remember is being at the Ritz in Paris and some ridiculously fancy pad in Biarritz on the French Riviera wondering how the hell I ended up in these places when I felt so unworthy——not to mention ugly, fat, and "slutty" (the word then for those of us who were a little more precocious than most)—time for another drink. I think we did another unchaperoned trip to the Bahamas, on which I got drunk, disappeared, and spent the night on the beach with some good looking blond guy I picked up.

I wasted an inordinate amount of time comparing myself to Jay and developed a habit of thinking that everyone, especially her, was so much better off than I. Not ever did I think that I might have been just as pretty, talented, or had anything to offer the world. I was progressively falling down the rabbit hole of self-hate and would continue to do so for many years to come.

I did manage to graduate from Hewitt's in 1966. I don't remember much of that year except for going out to Trader Vic's on Fridays after school, with my friends (in our school uniforms), and drinking Mai Tai's (rum and fruit juices), eating chochos and spareribs, and smoking cigarettes. I was dating yet another guy who was going to a university in Pennsylvania. I went down to visit him at his fraternity for the weekend, went to a beer bash, got smashed, and woke up at another university at a frat house with some guy I had never seen before. (Well, he was VERY cute, after all). Further down the rabbit hole.

The only place I applied for college was Sarah Lawrence (for music). One would have thought that I might have gotten in, as my grandfather had a great deal of influence there; but no—another blow to my already battered self-image. I ended up going to Finch College in New York City and majoring in music. Tricia Nixon was in my Botany class; that's all I remember of that experience. That lasted for one semester until I found the solution to all my problems...get married.

Song #10—*Soul For Sale*

CHAPTER THREE
The Disillusionment of Cinderella

I met the boy/man, Jimmy, who was to be my first husband, when I was 17. This was also the year of my debutante parties and "coming out" (coming out of what, I'm not sure). I opted to take a trip to Acapulco with six of my friends rather than have a private debutante party. Jimmy came with me for part of it.

I also was "presented" (to society) at a group cotillion in New York City. This should have been an exciting, joyful time of my life; but I was increasingly uncomfortable in my own skin and didn't have a clue as to who I was or what I wanted to do with the rest of my life. I bought the widespread myth that I could find myself through hooking up with Prince Charming, so I blinded myself to Jimmy's obvious faults and proceeded on my journey towards wedded bliss. He embellished his image with stories of partially true accomplishments; and most members of my family (and I) were all suitably impressed. Most people thought we were way too young; but, unfortunately, when you're way too young for something, you're not old enough to know that you're too young. We were engaged when I was 18 and married by the time I was 19.

Our wedding was very large and very elaborate. It was written up in the *New York Times* as every good socialite should want. I married him not once but twice. He was Catholic and I was a sort-of Episcopal, so we got married in both churches. The first lap of our honeymoon was to Edinburgh, Scotland where Jimmy was supposed to have attended pre-med school. Why he would go to a place where he knew I would find out he had lied is beyond me. But it was there that I first began to witness the unraveling of a whole web of lies. The second lap of the honeymoon was spent at the Ritz in Paris, visiting my grandmother, Bunny (Evie). I was in her good graces then and Jimmy managed to "snow" even her.

Returning to New York and being faced with the reality of married life with this man was a major shock. He didn't seem capable of holding a job, had not finished college as he had professed he had done, and generally did nothing to help out. I had since gone to Katherine Gibbs Secretarial School and started working at Macy's Architectural Department. I would return home in the evenings to a messy apartment, with Jimmy just sitting around more often than not. Both of us drank way too much.

Approximately one month after we got married, my father died of a heart attack at the age of 63. I felt nothing, literally nothing. I knew there was something wrong with my reaction, but at that time I still didn't feel safe enough to take the lid off Pandora's box. I did the only thing I knew how to do. I got drunk. I got so drunk I woke up the next morning in a pool of my own vomit. I'm surprised I didn't die because I remember choking on it.

A while later, we had a memorial service for him. Jimmy was unaccustomed to not being the center of attention. He threw one of his tantrums, picked a fight with me and caused so much chaos I thought I would lose my mind.

When I buried my father, I never thought about him again until my mother died sixteen years later. He ceased to exist for me. But unbeknownst to me, his constant psychic presence was anything but dead and drove me almost to suicide many times over the next few years.

My marriage was crumbling from the beginning. I was scared about our life, scared about not being good enough for my job, scared for my future, and clueless about how to navigate my own life, never mind a relationship. My solution was to get pregnant. It was not a happy pregnancy, as I kind of knew the marriage wasn't going to survive. I was very uneducated about pregnancy, childbirth and childrearing. Basically, I was doing it all on my own with no help or advice from anyone. When I went into labor, I didn't even know what was going on. I just thought I had to go to the bathroom really badly. My sister, Sally, was waiting for me outside the delivery room. Jimmy was out duck hunting or something like that.

My son, James Robertson Donaldson IV (Jamy), was born on February 4, 1969. When I brought him home from the hospital, I went into a postpartum depression without really knowing what that was. I was terrified at the enormity of bringing this child into the world and the responsibility that entailed. He was kind of colicky and cried a lot. My milk didn't appear to be sufficient for him, and I was getting more and more miserable in my relationship with Jimmy. Looking back on it, I feel sad for Jamy having to come into such an unhappy environment. Not a good beginning for him—no wonder he cried a lot. He was probably picking up on all the unexpressed feelings in the atmosphere. Less than a month later, after dinner at the swanky restaurant, "21", I turned 21 and left Jimmy just in time to inherit what little money I did inherit from my grandfather.

I moved back in with my mother for about six months. During that period, there were several incidents where I had to run out the back door of the apartment and go down the service elevator with the baby because Jimmy was pounding on the front door threatening to harm me. One time, he actually took Jamy and wouldn't bring him back, so I had to call the police. I was grateful at that time to have a place to stay and to have the help of Mummy's maids and cook, as I didn't have a clue how to take care of all the chores and him. Finally, I had to find a place of my own, and I moved into a small apartment on East 73rd Street. Talk about lonely. Oh my God, the first time living on my own with a little baby—no way out. I had to go to Mexico to get my divorce and ended up having to pay Jimmy's share of the expenses as well as my own. This was the beginning of the pattern of allowing myself to be divested of my money.

During this solo time, I dated a little bit. Maybe I should amend that to read that I went out to bars and periodically picked up someone. I also rekindled the romance with the older guy from when I was 16. He was in the process of a divorce, and we were hot and heavy for a while, until I realized he was a jerk and dumped him (revenge is sweet!).

I wasn't single long before I had a blind date with the man who was to become my second husband, Peter. I fell madly in love with him on the first date. He was from England and was attending Columbia Business School where he met a friend of my brother's from Vietnam. They thought it would be a good match, and it was...for a while, at least.

Peter was very good-looking, had an English accent and wore bikini underpants (a fact which I mistakenly identified as being bohemian). I think part of the reason I was attracted to him was because he was from another culture (born in Australia and raised in England). Perhaps I hoped he would take me away from my culture and into something more exciting. Little did I know he was trying to get into my social set and that he would be climbing up the social ladder as I was climbing down. He went from wearing bikini underpants to Pierre Cardin suits and boxers. His beautiful English accent soon faded as did anything remotely exotic about him. Bummer. At the time, I didn't consider my superficial criteria for selecting a suitable mate. Anyway, within two weeks, he was living with Jamy and me in my apartment.

We became a family scene quickly, and I was relatively happy, although something must have been going on, because we split up for a few months and then got back together. I found out he had started to date another woman and I couldn't stand it. I asked him to come back.

Shortly thereafter, we got married at a small ceremony at my mother's house in Locust Valley, Long Island. I drank so many whiskey sours I had to be carried to the limousine to go to the airport for our honeymoon. Peter spent the night in our airport hotel bathroom reading *Deliverance*—not an auspicious start to our new life. I had the worst hangover I had ever had when we landed in Paris. After Paris, we spent the second part of our honeymoon in Ethiopia, visiting Peter's parents who were living there at the time.

Upon our return, we moved out of my little apartment on East 73rd Street and bought a beautiful co-op on 95th and Park Avenue (moving up in the world).

I enrolled in some classes at the New School for Social Research, a very progressive college down near Greenwich Village. I took a class called "Consciousness Expansion" which, (looking back now), was the first step of a very long, spiritual search (in which Peter had no interest whatsoever). I started doing yoga, standing on my head, wearing beaded vests, and was verging on becoming a hippie (which is pretty hard to do when you're supposed to be a socialite living on Park Avenue). I smoked my first joint at the loft of a Chilean artist who was a friend of my sister, Barbara, and her husband, Luis (Cuban). The mixture of pot and drinking for me was not a good one, so I didn't do much of it. I did it enough, however, to end up with a bad batch once that made me sick and paranoid, and I ended up in the emergency room. I think it might have been laced with something else. That was that for a while.

In 1971, I became pregnant with my second child. This was a happier pregnancy than my first one, and I wasn't as scared the second time around. My daughter, Stephanie Mannering Thompson, was two weeks late and had to be induced. This time, my sister, Sally, was at a Mets game with my husband—hmmm... Peter did make it back in time for the actual birth and out came this beautiful little girl on June 28, 1972.

I probably haven't mentioned the fact that we had two St. Bernards in our apartment, partly paper trained. So, with two kids, two dogs and two of us in a New York City apartment... time to move.

When Stephanie was a month old and Jamy 3 years old, we moved from New York City and up to a farm in Cooperstown, New York. Peter's sister, Sarah, lived with us for the summer and helped us out. By the time she left to go back to England, we had six dogs (one of them only had three legs), veal calves, four horses, a couple of cows, and a bunch of chickens, plus the two kids. I (with much help from Peter and Sarah) took care of the horses, baled hay, learned how to dig postholes with a posthole digger, cleaned the dog pen, broke my rib falling on a wheelbarrow full of dog poop, scraped and wallpapered the inside of our farmhouse, and tried to raise my two kids.

We were all still drinking New York, social-set style. When Sarah finally left, Peter and I were left to our own devices and the consequences of our decision to become farmers. Neither one of us was cut out for farming, nor did we realize what a huge amount of work it was. After about a year, even all the distractions of trying to run a farm couldn't hide the fact that the marriage wasn't working. At the time, I really didn't know how to communicate what was going on with me, nor did he. Enter Sergio.

CHAPTER FOUR
So Much for White Picket Fences

Sergio was a dashing, Cuban man who had been an usher in my first wedding to Jimmy. He came to visit, we fell madly in love, and I left a month later to start a new life with him.

I don't regret leaving Peter because I don't think we had anything in common and we were headed down different roads. I do, however, regret the way I went about it. I think it devastated him at the time, and I almost lost Stephanie because of it. His reaction to the whole thing was to start a relationship with my sister, Sally, very shortly thereafter. He eventually moved back to the city and in with her. At one point, they were actually contemplating marriage.

During the period of our divorcing, he did threaten to go for full custody of Stephanie and used the tactic of accusing me of being "crazy like my mother" and being an unfit mother myself. Unable to stand up for myself, I accepted his perception of me and ended up essentially giving him everything that I had bought in the first place: the farm, all my furniture and my mother's antiques, Mercedes, Toyota Land Cruiser, etc. I walked out of there with the clothes on my back, my piano, and my kids.

Looking back on it, had I not felt so guilty for leaving, I would have fought harder to hang onto what was rightfully mine. If I had known he would end up making millions of dollars and living in Greenwich, Connecticut, I might have thought twice about letting him get away with most of my inheritance. However, I didn't, and he did, and there you have it. I was free.

Sergio and I spent the first couple of months of our relationship in a lean-to at Adirondack Lodge in Lake Placid. I'm pretty sure he was the love of my life. Whereas both my husbands and previous boyfriends had been the choice of my conditioning, Sergio was the choice of my heart. I had never felt that way before, or since, and it is the one relationship I always go back to and wonder what would have happened had it worked out. It was the first time I had felt anyone inside my soul and felt that sense of oneness that all the major spiritual traditions talk about. He played the guitar and serenaded me in Spanish and was absolutely irresistible to me. He was wonderful with the kids and adored them as they adored him. He really wanted kids of his own and treated them as if they were his own. He was kind, open, loving, and affectionate and unlike anyone I had ever known. And he loved me like I had never been loved.

Song #11—*Freefall*

We rented a house in the town of Lake Placid and opened a record/8-track tape store in Saranac Lake. Our relationship revolved mostly around music. When not working in the store (usually with the kids), we would listen to all sorts of music (especially John Denver) at night. We eventually bought a piece of property out on the lake and moved out there. The only bad thing about this whole scene was that we both drank way too much. It was like the Days of Wine and Roses. As much as I loved him, I began to be aware of this tremendous reservoir of pain in me, and I didn't know what to do about it.

Something in me began to get restless and increasingly self-destructive. I was unaccustomed to this much intimacy (and probably a whole lot of codependence). Consequently, I split up with him in absolute misery, not knowing what was propelling me away from someone that I loved so much.

When Sergio moved out, I was left to myself with two small children, living out in the middle of nowhere. For a while, I kept the store going by myself, but finally had to let it go. I was very lonely way out in the middle of nowhere and felt overwhelmed trying to raise the kids on my own. There was a short period where I drank a bottle of wine every night and cried myself to sleep. I ended up sleeping with a couple of men I never would have slept with, had I not been totally drunk.

On New Year's Day 1974, I woke up with a guy (we actually didn't do anything) after a night of drinking and eating pot brownies, and I knew that if I kept on going this way, I was going to be dead by the time I was 30. I called a friend of mine who I knew went to AA and asked him to take me to a meeting. He did, and except for one night ten years later, I have not had another drink since.

The night of my first AA meeting, after I went home, I had my first of many "mystical" experiences. I sat down at the piano and the entire *Rhapsody in Blue* played through me in a way I had never played it even when at the top of my form. I say "played through me" because my eyes were closed and I hadn't touched a piano in about ten years. This experience was to carry me through some even darker times to come and was, unbeknownst to me, a precursor to many other mystical, musical experiences in my future. For about a year after that, I listened to a song by Eric Clapton called *Let it Grow*, and that, combined with the *Rhapsody* experience, gave me the strength to keep growing.

Song #12—*Unsung Heroes*

Sergio and I tried to get back together, as we still had passionate feelings for each other. Unfortunately, he was still drinking and we just couldn't make it work. As I am writing this, I still have sadness when I think about it. Had I known then what I know now, perhaps I could have hung in there because he ultimately did quit drinking. He eventually did remarry and did have a child of his own, so perhaps it worked out for the best. I felt sad for the kids, too, because as young as they were, they were still very attached to him.

Soon after the failed attempt to get back with Sergio, I started dating a guy named Tom. Although I was still sober at this point, Tom was not, and was into drugs as well. This relationship was short-lived, and I started dating Tom's friend, Dick (aptly named and also a heavy drinker and into drugs) (and no, Dick did not have a friend named Harry). I was also dating another man named Dan who was actually a good man, and he wanted to marry me. But for some reason, I chose Dick over him.

I didn't understand it at the time, but I substituted my obsession with drinking with a drinker. This relationship was the closest to an abusive one that I have ever been in. Dick gave me much grief about my not drinking anymore, was physically scary, and sexually kinky. I didn't think I had any options but to do as he wanted, so I allowed myself to be bullied into things I wouldn't normally have done. At the time, I wasn't aware of my incest issues. I just know I did not have the power to say no.

Dick moved in with the kids and me for a short period. He was not good with kids. They didn't like him, and I regret ever having brought him into their lives. During that time, I had to have a total hysterectomy (no coincidence there). When I got out of the hospital, he was on my case to cook his dinners and give him the sex that he required, with no regard for my physical health. It was then that it began to dawn on me that this guy was a "creep." So I kicked him out.

A little while after I got rid of him, a man broke into my house in the middle of the night and jumped in bed with me. He was very drunk and very big (6' 5"/250 lb.). After about a half hour, I talked him into letting me go to the bathroom and called the police. I then went into the kitchen and pulled a knife out of the drawer and was contemplating stabbing him, but knew the kids were sleeping and didn't want to cause them any more trauma (I was remarkably calm at the time). By that time, he had cornered me in the kitchen, and he was drunk enough that I managed to get him out the back door and locked it. Then he went around to all the other doors and windows and was banging on them. The police finally came and took him away.

I ended up having to face him in court where his lawyer tried to turn the tables on me by saying I had invited him in for a drink in my slinky nightie (I did not drink at all by then, nor did I own a slinky nightie). Anyway, this was one of those classic cases of blaming the victim. He got away with a fine of $300. I had trouble sleeping for the next 25 years.

All this was so traumatic, I moved back into town and actually got back together with Dick for a short time. I also had to have another major surgery (gall bladder removed because I had seventeen gall stones at the tender age of 29). I had one final, triumphant break-up with Dick (he was yelling out his car window "No one will ever love you as much as I do."—yuk), and I walked away, never to look back.

Song #13—*You're Not the Cure*

In walks Andrew (Andy). Andy was the sweetest person I had ever met in my life. He was also ten years younger than I (I was 30 and he was 20). I was still experiencing a huge amount of pain, and by this time I was so paranoid about living with anyone that even when he just left his shoes at my house, I would freak out. We were together for about a year; and again I had some very happy times. My kids thought he was great (he was as much older than them as I was than him), and we all had a lot of fun water skiing and listening to the Doobie Brothers while driving around in his car.

After a while, though, the age difference started to get to me, and I ended it. He started dating a girl his own age; and once again, I lost it. Only this time I didn't marry him as I did my second husband. This time I lost my mind, literally.

I felt my mind snap, and I entered into a period of about a year-and-a-half-long, dark night of the soul. I couldn't eat. I couldn't sleep. I couldn't work. I couldn't cry. I couldn't feel. The one thing I remember to this day is the very weird experience of my life coming to a screaming halt and being very aware that life went on without me. Everyone else was on the merry-go-round of life, and for some reason, I had stepped off, and it didn't seem to be a conscious choice. I tried an anti-depressant for about a month, but it made me feel like a zombie. I got a hold of some quaaludes and took them for sleeping, but those didn't work either. Somehow I could go through the motions of taking care of my kids, but mentally I had left the planet. (I am well aware as I write this book that my kids can sometimes seem incidental to the story. Nothing could be further from the truth. That is a whole new book that will probably get written sometime in the future). All this went on for what seemed like an eternity.

Song #14—*Even Here*

I didn't know at the time that I was going through a process of detoxing, physically and emotionally, from giving up drinking, and early menopause from my hysterectomy. Also, I had been practicing and teaching yoga for quite a long time and was unaware of kundalini, chakras, and other modes of consciousness. Looking back on this period, I would say that it was more of a breakthrough than a breakdown. But I did not, unfortunately, have that information at the time and would not until many years later. It scared the hell out of me.

I finally went to visit my mother (who had a hard time holding onto her own sanity) in Santa Barbara, California. This trip proved to be a turning point in my life (coincidentally, I had just seen the movie *Turning Point* with Anne Bancroft and Shirley MacLaine), and in fact, completely altered the trajectory of my life. I was initiated by my stepsister into TM (Transcendental Meditation) and began what would be a life-long meditative practice and spiritual search. I returned for a short time to Lake Placid, where I then felt like a fish out of water, and moved my kids and myself out to Santa Barbara. A whole new chapter...

EVIE THOMPSON (EVIE T.)

ON THE EDGE

On the edge
of night
and day
where vaporous
dreams mock
waking hearts
I laid me
down
to cry
for ways
I had to
leave behind
and friends
who could not
follow me
for pasts
ripped from
my desperate hands
to let
the girl
who lived
in me
slip through
the grasp
of yesterday
and felt
the void
envelope me
as I emptied
into darkness

a moan of
human hopelessness
screamed across
the endless space
between my bed
and hell
the arms
of God
reached down
for me
and held me
til I
filled again
a child had died
a woman
freed
to face
an unknown
destiny.

CHAPTER FIVE
Sleeping Beauty Starts to Wake Up

Moving to California wasn't a quick fix for my problems; but it sure did open some doors and give me a sense of freedom that the East Coast social scene couldn't. I spent a lot of time at the TM center in Santa Barbara, taking classes to raise my consciousness, and I meditated daily. I had many more mystical experiences, and it was the first time in my life that I felt this whole new world and inner light inside of me. I met many interesting people who were pretty far out by my standards, but I loved it. I hung out at the Miramar Hotel and met people like Jimmy Messina (Loggins and Messina) who really triggered my creative urges by just being around him (at that time it manifested as poetry). I roller skated on the bike paths in my bikini, got toe rings in Venice Beach, and was introduced to nude hot-tubbing at Esalan in Big Sur. I had a wonderful fling with the son of one of my mother's friends who was ten years younger, (and this would become a pattern) and was a singer/guitar player.

During the two years I spent in Santa Barbara, I finished my degree in Counseling Psychology and began work on a Masters Degree. When I shared my joy at getting my college degree with my mother, her reaction was, "I could have done that." That was the first time I actually said anything to her about that particular competitive behavior of hers, and she did not take it well. By that time, her health was declining, so

I didn't say much more than that. But, basically, it was a good two years and I value the time I got to spend with her. I didn't really know then that she only had a little time left.

My grandmother, Bunny, died right before I moved to Santa Barbara. I experienced very little grief because she had cut me off and cut me out of her will sometime before that, which actually hurt more than her death.

Then in 1982, my brother-in-law, Luis, killed himself. He called my sister, Barbara (they were divorced by then) before he died, hoping she could save him; but the EMTs got to him after she did, and he died in her arms. We all loved Luis and were devastated. I dreamed about him constantly over the next few years. He instructed me in piano in almost all the dreams (he was a talented pianist while in his body). I also had a rather bizarre incident one time when I felt like I channeled a message from him to be delivered to Barbara. At the time, everyone thought I was nuts: but looking back on it, it was the first of many encounters with the invisible world.

I had two very significant dreams during this period. One was a very clear message to move to the mountains. The other was a white screen with big black letters that said "Physician, heal thyself." I don't know whether I should have taken these dreams quite as literally as I did, but I did. In the summer of 1982, my kids and I moved to Lake Tahoe. Had I known my mother would die within a year and a half, I might have waited until she was gone. But the kids and I fell in love at first sight with Lake Tahoe and off we went. We were visiting my friends, Marcia and Jon, who we had known in Lake Placid. We spent one night with them, went back to Santa Barbara and moved one month later to a house we had never seen.

My mother died in the early part of 1984. I had no concept of what it would be like to have my mother die. I went into a state of shock for a while, so much so that I didn't even remember being at the funeral or where the grave was when I went back to Santa Barbara a few years later. I dreamed about her all the time for years, and in many of those dreams, she would come back to life. She almost died so many times while I was growing up that I didn't quite believe it when she actually did. The few things I do remember were: telling her it was okay for her to go; having her last words to me be, "Poor Eve" (I never did figure out what she meant by that); and the time she grabbed me and pulled me down so she could whisper, "Do I have to forgive him?" (meaning, my stepfather), to which I said, "Yes."

Later that same year, at Christmas, I took the kids over to visit my sister, Sally, in London. We spent New Year's Eve in Inverness, Scotland, with her boyfriend's family, and on New Year's Day we received a call that my stepfather, Peter, had died. I will never forget hearing Sally screaming all the way up the stairs as she came to tell me. We went to Long Island, New York, for the funeral. By that time, we were all totally traumatized.

Somewhere in there (I'm not sure what year) Sally's best friend, Ann Clouet, from France, died at a very young age of cancer. Anne lived with us for quite a while, so we were all close to her.

By this time, I had just shut down, because I was trying to raise my kids on my own and was working full-time. One of the ways I chose to deal with all these blows was to not deal with it. I decided I would become obsessed with yet another guitar player (my daughter's guitar teacher) and diligently attempted to meditate myself out into the ozone. I got very good at out-of-body experiences.

At the time, I wrote a book of poems called "Whispers"

EVIE THOMPSON (EVIE T.)

(see title poem below). Ten years later, when a dear friend of mine died at the age of 52, and I began to be able to deal with it all, I wrote:

Song #15—*No Goodbyes*

<u>Whispers</u>

If only
I could remember
what you looked like,
I could paint
another picture
and hang it
on my brain.

If only
I could remember
what you sounded like,
I could stop
the noisy past
and listen
to myself.

If only
I could remember
what you felt like
I could let go
of fear
and hold myself.

If only
you were all around me,
I could breathe
in deeply
and make you
part of me.

If only
I could fill this hole
that you have left
and have another
chance at growing up.

If only
I could have
all of me
in one place
at the same time
I could go forward.

So I close my eyes
and try to see you
hold up my arms
and hope that you are there
listen for your whispers
to tell me it's ok
and breathe...you back to life in me.

CHAPTER SIX
Follow the Yellow Brick Road

Shortly after all of this, I opened a bookstore (Reed and Boggs Book Merchants) in Tahoe City, with my friend, Marcia. I wasn't really into the retail thing (you would have thought I would have figured that out after the record store!), but I wasn't quite sure what I wanted to be when I grew up, so I guess it served its purpose.

My favorite section of books was the metaphysical section. I read every book I could get my hands on. One of my favorites was Shirley MacLaine's *Out on a Limb*. I wrote to her and she wrote me back—which I thought was terribly exciting. At the same time, I had joined a group of people studying *A Course in Miracles*. I wasn't exactly sure what it actually said; I only know it had a huge impact on my life.

Sometime in 1983, my guitar-playing boyfriend introduced me to two friends of his in Sausalito who owned a recording studio and happened to be looking for some additional backing and a new partner. I just happened to have inherited some money when my mother died, and without much thought, I found myself the third partner in the studio. Shortly thereafter, Craig went back to his old girlfriend and married her. I was devastated and hung on to the illusion of what we never had for years—a great way to avoid reality.

Song #16—*Puppet on a String*

By this time, however, I was smartening up and started asking myself, "Why, for God's sake, was I clinging to this person who was obviously totally wrong for me?" Finally, after sending him money to help him and his new wife out (have I mentioned that I had a pattern of giving all my money away to the men in my life? Or at least buying them cars?), I figured it out. He was a musician. I had fallen in love with a part of myself that I had totally disowned.

I hadn't planned it when I first became involved with the studio, but I ended up writing and recording my first two albums there. *Going Home Again* was a collection of solo piano pieces, and *Keeping Me Company* was a collection of pop-rock songs with lyrics and the first time I started to sing. The first of these songs to come to me woke me up in the middle of the night. It was called *Angels Don't Sleep*.

Song #17—*Angels Don't Sleep*

I think, at the time, I completely misunderstood the lyrics to the song and didn't have a clue that it was actually about angels. Even though there is an angel on the cover, it took quite a few years before I knew there really <u>were</u> angels and that I had many of them around me AND they loved music! I do realize, of course, that many people consider a belief in angels to be bordering on lunacy. I thought so, too, at the time, but I have since been made a believer. Happily so, I might add.

At the same time I was traveling back and forth to the Bay Area (by then Marcia and I had sold the bookstore), I was now raising two teenagers and going to school full-time for a degree in music.

During those years, my kids had a few of their friends who stayed with us for varying lengths of time. This was not an easy time for any of us. Jamy and I seemed to be in constant battles and power struggles (I came to find out that it is relatively normal during the teenage years), and it's a wonder we all made it out alive. I was having major problems juggling being a mother with forging my own path. It certainly would have been easier had I forged my own path before I had kids; but no-o-o...I was going through my own adolescent growing pains at the same time they were. At one point, we all had punk hairdos at the same time. Not your typical mother, I'm sure. Add to that my rather bizarre spiritual pursuits and I can imagine that it wasn't too easy being an offspring of mine.

Before I got out of the studio business, I had one more exceedingly dysfunctional relationship with yet another dysfunctional musician (by that time, I had figured out I was the common denominator) whom I supported for a period of time. My partnership in the studio ended at about the same time as my relationship with this man; and, unfortunately for me, ended in a lawsuit in which I turned out to be the major loser. Even though we went to mediation, they only ended up paying me half of what they owed me. We're talking a huge amount of money that was a large percentage of what I had inherited.

My life at this stage was a curious mix of destiny and dysfunction, and it's hard to tell where one left off and the other began. I definitely knew I was following some kind of higher vision that was way beyond me, and at the same time I was having all these ridiculously dysfunctional dramas going on.

Jamy graduated from high school in 1987 and went off

to a junior college in San Diego and then on to University Colorado at Boulder. Right before he left, I bought a house in Tahoe City, which was to be my home for the next 13 years.

After swearing I would never have another pet, I ended up with two new dogs (supposedly for the kids), Coors and Snickers—a golden retriever and a chocolate lab (guess which one is which?!). These dogs were like my adopted children, and I had a wonderful time mountain biking with them running beside me.

Also in the late 1980s, I began in earnest to deal with my alcoholic family and molestation issues. I went to therapy, 12-step programs, and other personal growth programs, and slowly but surely began my ascent out of the hell that had been the first part of my life. I explored many different spiritual paths including (but not limited to):

Christianity:
Song #18—*Now That Jesus is My Friend*
Song #19—*Walk on the Water*

Native American:
Song #20—*The Indian Way*

Japanese (Mahikari):
Song #21—*Children of the Sun*

Shamanism:
Song #22—*Call of the Wild*

New Age/Religious Science/Unity:
Song #23—*The Better it Gets*

Eastern (Art of Living):
Song #24—*Voyagers to Love*

Through all my explorations, the common thread for me seemed to be music, personal growth and the search for the commonalities between all the different religions/paths. I suppose some people might have labeled me a dilettante; but in fact, I was on some kind of personal mission, and my path seems to have been one of many paths—with my music the common denominator.

Stephanie graduated in 1990 and also went off to Boulder. I sang at her graduation.

Song #25—*You've Got it All*

Empty-nest syndrome threw me for a loop. One child gone was a relief, but both gone—'oy vay.' And of course, what did I do? Yup, yet another dysfunctional relationship (yes, he played guitar) with a man named Roland. Roland was an engineer and a private pilot. We had a whole lot of fun for a very short period of time and then all hell broke loose. He had two kids from a previous marriage and was very obviously looking for someone who was going to be a substitute mother. As desperate as I was, I was not about to go through all that again, so the whole relationship blew up (on a trip to Death Valley, I might add).

One of the most interesting happenings during that relationship was the time I was looking at him and all of a sudden this kaleidoscope of the various men in my life (father, stepfather, brother, husbands, boyfriends, etc.) superimposed itself over his face and I couldn't see him anymore. I came away thinking either he WAS a conglomeration of the best and the worst of all the men in my life or I was projecting all of that onto him. In either case, I knew it was time for celibacy (twelve years so far!).

YOU WERE...
A MAN

We were
separate
you and I
from the moment
I was born
a line was
drawn between
our worlds
we could not cross
nor touch nor understand.
You were...
an alien patriarch
ruling from the distance
our planets collided for
fleeting instants
of tumultuous
fumbling contacts
the aftershocks
of which would hurl us
both whimpering
to the farthest
corners of our
isolated universes
to lick our wounds and
prepare for the next collision.

You were...
a gifted fabricator weaving
lovely fiendish
tapestries of lies
to woo me
trick me smother me
ruin me
but I kept on breathing
and ran away draggin' with me
the pieces of
a shattered illusion and
slowly dying innocence.
You were...
a charming symbiont
feeding off my strength
draining me of all I had
to give until
I could not bear
the burden of us both
nor of myself
I crawled away
on hands and knees
and quietly lost my mind.
You were...
a dignified sadist
attempting to finish
the job that others
had started
of bringing me down
in spite of your skilled
inflictions of
inner and outer pain

I found my mind
my voice my self
I stood in anger
and proudly limped away.
You were…
a tender fledgling
who could not comprehend
the pain in my eyes
the fear in my flight
nor the wall
around my heart
but knew enough
to hold me gently
until the trembling stopped.
You were…
both a god and demon
a giant and a dwarf
a concrete apparition
that came and went
as I went and came
we could not see each other then
but now I think I glimpse a little
of who you really are.
you are a man
no more no less
a person much like me.

Right after the breakup, Stephanie moved home and
moved in with her boyfriend, Derrek. Derrek had lost both his
father and his brother within a year or so, and she felt the need
to be closer to him.

During this period of time, I started working on a pilot's license (not to be outdone by Roland), and doing wild things such as skydiving and bungee jumping. I did get my pilot's license, which was a major accomplishment, but I haven't flown since because of an inner ear condition and vertigo that developed as a result of all the altitude shifts.

This was further complicated by the fact that I was experiencing flashbacks and memories from all the inner work I was doing with the molestations and other childhood traumas. I had difficulty sleeping and woke up many mornings choking. It was a little hard to sort out what was what at that point. I only know I threw up for three years straight and still do occasionally when I am triggered in any way by anything remotely resembling revictimization or when my fear becomes too overwhelming.

After one particularly horrendous winter in Tahoe, I decided to move to Los Angeles in September 1992. Right before I left, Stephanie had the first of a series of blood clots that she would have over the next several years. This one was a pulmonary embolism. It was a major challenge for me to move and leave her behind, but by that time she and Derrek were living in my house and I had enrolled in UCLA's songwriting program—so I went. Five months and one earthquake, several major fires, mudslides, and race riots later, I moved back.

I didn't actually finish the songwriting program, but I made a valuable connection there through one of the teachers who brought me into his studio where I met the man, David Vasquez, who was to be my musical partner for the next thirteen years and eight albums.

I couldn't sleep in Los Angeles for about a year after the earthquake. I flew down to Los Angeles once a month for about a year and David would pick me up at the Burbank Airport for a day of recording, then put me on the last flight back. Slowly but surely I felt safe enough to spend a night or two and ended up staying with my sister, Barbara, who was living down there at the time.

Song #26—*Metamorphosis*
Song #27—*Wings of Change*

CHAPTER SEVEN
All That Glitters…

Song #28—*All the Lights in Hollywood*

I didn't realize (until I spent some amount of time in Los Angeles and was surrounded by it) how much I had bought into the fame game. I suppose if I had REALLY wanted to be famous I could have been. Unfortunately (or perhaps fortunately) I had a huge part of me working in the opposite direction. After growing up in a famous family, I think I had made an unconscious decision to be as obscure as I possibly could be. The part of me that didn't want to be famous and the part of me that did were in constant battle. A musician, to some extent, has to be visible in order to deliver the gifts somewhere. As much as I loved playing, writing, singing, and recording music, performance was more of a chore than anything. I spent years performing publicly, all the while trying to figure out how to be a singer and songwriter without actually having to perform. (This book solves that problem!).

I had to spend much time soul-searching as to the purpose of my doing music and about the kind of life I wanted to live as a musical artist. One of the songs I wrote during that questioning period was called *Light up the Stars.*

Song #29—*Light up the Stars*

It has been difficult to uproot all the family programming related to my chosen path. The message I got was that it was okay to be an artist of some sort as long as you were a famous artist and made piles of money. Being a teacher or a dedicated, relatively unknown artist didn't quite make the cut ("not QUITE top-drawer" as my grandmother used to say). Those kind of disparaging inner voices have plagued me my whole musical career. Never mind that I got a degree in music, wrote and recorded nine albums of original music, learned how to apply the computer to my musical pursuits, taught publicly and privately, performed all over the place, and on and on... none of those counted in the kingdom of the Fields.

I have never felt that I measured up or that what I have achieved is good enough for one lifetime. This whole struggle has abated somewhat over the last few years, thank God, and I can now appreciate the value of all my work. But, oh my, what a long road it has been to get to that point. And I am subject to relapse on this issue.

During most of the 1990s, I worked as a Music Director at a Religious Science church in Tahoe. Religious Science is a philosophy/way of life based on the teachings of Ernest Holmes. Basically, it teaches that there is a universal force that we can all tap into to create the kind of life we desire, i.e., "you create your own reality" (a saying that later started to drive me nuts and can be used to beat yourself over the head if anything less than perfection manifests in your life). I was more interested in doing music than anything having to do with the teachings, but for a while I was a very dedicated student of the whole thing.

Interestingly enough, I came up against the same kind of thinking as in my family—bigger is better, more of everything, you're not doing it right if you're not making a ton of money, you don't count if you're not famous, etc. So the famous, not famous battle raged on for me for another few years. One thing that really annoyed me about the whole thing was that it was all too easy to use the "positive thinking" aspect to further suppress any so-called "negative" feelings or thoughts I might be feeling or thinking. Don't get me wrong, I think it is much better to be an optimistic, forward-looking, happy person than it is to be a pessimistic, backward-looking, miserable person. There is a fine line, however, between making the best out of life's difficulties and slipping into a state of denial. I saw many people who were so focused on the "Light" they neglected to notice they were dragging a huge shadow-self behind them.

Song #30—*Shadowboxing*

The upside of the job was that it served as sort of a cradle for my musical endeavors and the whole experience did really contribute to my inner knowing that God was not some external, far-off patriarch in the sky. In some ways I do think we create our own reality, but not in the simplistic way that some of the New Thought religions would have us believe. I think we all have our karma/baggage to work out, and as we do that (which is usually an enormous amount of sometimes very painful work), our lives and attitudes will change. But as far as I know, no one ever really escapes the nitty-gritty work part of it and spiritual bypasses don't work for long.

For me, my music was my way of dealing with my issues. At this time in my life, it was still hard for me to just have my feelings about things, so I would write songs, and all the emotions had a place to go. Almost every time I wrote a song, I was working on some issue; and by the end of the song, very often the issue would resolve itself to some extent. I ended up writing songs about everything—including my personal issues, other people's issues, death, love, politics, current events, tragedies, feminist issues, religious issues, anything that moved me.

I started to feel like a human jukebox. Push a button and out pops a song. It's a lovely talent, but so far I haven't gotten rich from it (who said that?!—must be my grandmother). Actually, it is only now, in the writing of this book, that I am beginning to appreciate what an amazing talent it is. Anything that could make something beautiful out of the hell that was my life, and help me heal from it all, is quite remarkable.

CHAPTER EIGHT
Kids, Kids, and More Kids

After I moved back from Los Angeles, I ended up living in my house with Derrek and Stephanie. I slept in Stephanie's old room and they slept in my room because they were still renting the house from me (role reversal). Jamy graduated from Boulder and he was home for a while, also. Stephanie and Derrek decided to get married in August 1994.

I went to a psychic who said Stephanie would tell me she was pregnant on May 1, 1994. I didn't say anything, and lo and behold, on April 30, I was walking in the parking lot and Steph drove up and said, "Guess what?", and I immediately said "You're pregnant." She was rather excited about the fact that a psychic told me, so she said to ask the psychic what sex it would be. The psychic was right again. So the marriage took place in August, and my grandson, Sean Connor, was born on January 11, 1995. I was present at the birth. UNBELIEVABLE.

Song #31—*Love Looking at Me*

By the time Connor was born, Steph and Derrek had bought a house. Not long after that, they began having financial problems and had to sell the house and move back in with me. So, I was now living with my daughter, her husband, my grandchild, their malamute, and my two dogs in a fairly small house. It was actually a wonderful experience and I cherish the time I had with them all in those close quarters. I, too, was beginning to have financial difficulties and was having trouble maintaining my house.

At one point when the married kids were living with me, and Jamy was being fed by Daddy Bruce and the Hare Krishna in Boulder, I started to get really upset about the inequity in the Field family money distribution. There was something oddly ironic about a granddaughter of Marshall Field not being able to pay for health insurance or able to send her son money for food.

As fate would have it, at the same time, an article about my family came out in Vanity Fair magazine. The slant of the article was predictably in favor of the males. My mother was mentioned, briefly, with no mention of the fact that she wrote two books on mental illness that helped a lot of people—one of which made the *New York Times* bestseller list for a brief period of time.

Also, as fate would have it again, the Biography Channel aired a program on my family—again, blatantly favoring the males. At one point in the program a picture of my mother, her sister, and her brother came on. The commentator said something to the effect that Marshall Field III had three children. The camera zoomed in on my uncle, and they cut my mother and aunt out of the picture, while continuing to talk about the accomplishments of the men.

After that, I wrote both of my male cousins (one was then a billionaire) and asked them if they could lend me the money to pay off my home equity loan ($85,000). One didn't answer at all, and the one that did (and I AM grateful to him) did lend me the money, but with it came a letter to never ask again and a lecture about running up my credit cards. I guess if you have 5 or 600 million dollars, you don't need to use your credit cards to pay your bills.

Anyway, I came away from the encounter feeling ashamed, incompetent, and inconsolably sad that my family didn't really care what happened to me. What he didn't realize, perhaps, was that I brought up two children on my own, with no help from one husband and very little from the second. Also, maybe he didn't realize how little we actually got and that no one bothered to teach us, or emulate for us, how to make as much as we reasonably needed or how to protect ourselves from people who would take what little we had.

Yes, I made a couple of unfortunate investments with the money I inherited, but pretty much everything I had went towards raising my kids, furthering my education, and doing my music. Not alot of extravagance and all worthy causes.

I was commiserating with my brother about the whole issue, and he said, "Basically, you don't matter." He wasn't saying that because he believed it, but because that was the reality of our family's attitude towards us. I tried to hang on to the house for the next few years, but even with the home equity loan paid off, I was getting deeper and deeper in the hole. I was still trying to collect on the money owed to me by the studio in Sausalito, and it cost me more money to hire a lawyer to keep after them.

Meanwhile, I was still going back and forth to Los Angeles to record, and spent some time on the road playing at Religious Science and Unity churches in California, Nevada, Colorado, and Wyoming. My dear friend, Kathy, from back East, was by then living in Boulder, so Boulder became a kind of second home for me. This was the year of the Oklahoma City bombing and my becoming more and more politically inclined.

Song #32—*Heartland*
Song #33—*Fascist Swing*

About a year and a half after my first grandchild was born, my second grandchild came. Her name was Sevannah. She was tiny compared to Connor. I remember I could hold her in the palms of my hands. I would have written a song for her, too, but right after she was born, Stephanie lost the feeling in the left side of her face. Thus began a series of events that would consume the next six months of our lives.

Steph had an MRI, and it was determined that she had an acoustic neuroma (brain tumor located on the acoustic nerve). In the process of administering the dye for the MRI, she ended up with a blood clot in her arm. The blood clot was the most dangerous of the two things at that time, so they put her back in the hospital after Sevannah's birth and kept her on blood thinners.

When her blood condition was deemed to be more stable a few months later, we all went down to Los Angeles and stayed with my sister, Barbara, so Steph could have the operation to have the tumor removed. There was the possibility after that kind of an operation that she could lose all the muscular control of that side of her face, but she didn't, thank God. She did, however, lose her hearing on that side, and still has periodic losses of equilibrium and constant ringing in her ears. She handled all of this—then and now—with amazing balance.

When she and Derrek got back on their feet after all this, they moved out and started to do really well financially. They both worked hard at building Derrek's contracting business; and it, and they, began to flourish.

I continued to go back and forth to Los Angeles, and by

the year 2000, I had written and recorded eight albums. Jamy was doing well in his career in the Bay Area, and life was fairly stable, creative, exciting, and with no major crises for a short period. This was a blessing because the year 2000 ended up being one of the hardest years of my life.

CHAPTER NINE
Heaven Can't Wait

In the last few months of 1999, I had to put both of my dogs to sleep. By then Coors was 13 and Snickers was 14. They weren't supposed to be my dogs, but of course I became totally attached to both of them. They were my best friends, usually my only constant companions, and I loved them both dearly. The vet came to the house for Coors and he died in my arms. I had probably waited a month too long in his case. I had been dragging him from room to room on a blanket because I just couldn't bear to part with him. Derrek's mom, Joann, came over to be with me, as she had just been through it with her dog. When the vet carried the lifeless body of my beloved golden retriever out that door, I thought I was going to lose it. I wrote a song for him and played it on a boom box as I scattered his ashes on the lake.

Song #34—*Dancing on the Wind*

Not long after that, Snickers started having terrible seizures where she appeared to die for a minute or so and then she would jump back up and run in circles, panting. The vet thought she had lesions on her brain. At first, the seizures were a long time apart; but then they started to get closer together. I knew it was time for her to go 'Home' as well, so I took her to the vet and she was put to sleep. Her last experience on this earth was of having cookies (anyone who knew her knew the importance of that), looking into my eyes and being held in my arms. I wrote her a song as well and played it as I scattered her ashes on the lake and in the woods.

Song #35—*Hurry Home*

I went through a few months of some very heavy grieving and swore I would never have another dog. In April 2000, I was just starting to come back to the land of the living. I had written some new songs and took a trip down to Los Angeles to record them and go to a spiritual retreat for a few days. Between those two activities, I was flying high. I felt so happy just to be alive and to be doing what I loved. On my way back from Los Angeles, I stopped in Santa Barbara and went to the Vedanta temple to meditate. While I was there, for some unknown reason I bought a beautiful rose quartz rosary. About a half an hour later I got a call on my cell phone that my sister, Sally, had been diagnosed with end-stage lung cancer which had also gone into her bones. I felt like someone had kicked me in the stomach, and all the joy I had been feeling just moments before was gone. I drove the rest of the way home in a fog. A few days later, Sally called and asked if I would take her dog, Puck. So much for no more dogs…

A few weeks after the news, I went back to Lake Placid for a reunion for all the people that used to hang out at a bar on the lake called The Cottage. We had all since scattered to the four winds. It was a fun trip in some ways but I was still in shock about Sally.

While I was back there, I was talking to my friend, Niki, about not wanting to have another dog. Somehow, she managed to help me see that even if I did take her, I didn't necessarily have to keep her after Sally died. So I decided when I went home, I would tell Sally I would take her.

I saw Sergio on this trip. It was kind of a disappointing meeting because I would like to have talked to him to maybe heal some things that happened between us. But it wasn't the time or the place, and his wife was with him. I felt some sadness when I left Lake Placid, for both the past and what I knew lay ahead.

In July of that year, Puck arrived at the San Francisco Airport, after having been in a cage for nineteen, hot hours. Jamy and I had to pick her up at 4:00 a.m. in a cargo building. Sally said she never barked, but as we got out of the car, we heard this loud, forlorn, and unceasing barking coming from the only dog cage around, so I assumed this was Puck. I went around to the front of the cage and I'll never forget her face right then. She looked totally freaked out and disoriented. I took her home to Tahoe and introduced her to the lake and the Truckee River. I was assuming she was a water dog, but she had apparently never seen water and didn't know what to do with it, so she just stood and drank like it was her very own big water bowl.

I made the mistake of leaving her home alone a few times and came back to find that she had literally dismantled and chewed my front door into kindling, chewed the ski boot bench, not to mention all the pillows on the couch. Someone had neglected to tell me she had abandonment issues. I almost gave her away right then, but someone suggested crate training her, so that seemed to work for the next four years, until I found out that she had a cancerous tumor, at which time she refused to get in the crate anymore. Needless to say, I fell madly in love with this rather high maintenance dog, and she has been a huge blessing in my life.

Between April of that year and the time Sally died on

December 24, 2000, I went back East to visit her three times. She was in some intense chemo and radiation therapy and was out of it most of the time. She wasn't drinking and was much sweeter than she had been when she was drinking, which made it all the harder.

A couple of my most poignant memories from that time included going to the movies with her to see *Remember the Titans*. I was crying all the way through it, and by the end, she was asleep. Her head had drooped to the side, and her wig had fallen to the side so that when she straightened up it was sitting sideways on her head. I kept trying to get it back on properly, but it seemed to bother me more than her. Another time, she was lying in her bed and I had an overwhelming urge to climb in bed with her, like I did when we were little; but I didn't do it because I thought she would get annoyed (which she probably would have). I tell you, though, if I ever have that urge again when someone I love is dying, I'm going to do it no matter what anyone else thinks.

I never heard her talk about the fact that she was dying. She wasn't into any spiritual stuff, but I had since given her the rose quartz rosary I had bought in Santa Barbara. She actually wore the beads all the time, but she had to take the cross off because it cut into her chemo shunt. The last time I left there was after I had gone back for her daughter's wedding. She seemed to hang on just for that. We went shopping to buy her a beautiful dress to wear, and we all made it through the wedding, celebrating the marriage and mourning her imminent death at the same time. When I left that time, I knew it would be the last time I would see her. That was around Thanksgiving 2000.

Around that time, I finally came to the realization that I could no longer hang onto my house in Tahoe, and I couldn't take one more winter with 20 feet of snow; so I sold my house to Steph and Derrek and moved down to Nevada City. I ended up renting an adorable, old Victorian house that belonged to Sally's ex-husband's sister.

On December 24, I was cooking Christmas Eve dinner in my new house (one of Sally's favorite meals of roast beef and Yorkshire pudding) when I had the urge to call her daughter, Kathy. Apparently, right after her kids had tucked her in for the night at the Hospice place and went home, she passed away. Even though I knew it was coming, I was stunned. As big a pain in the … as she could be, she was my sister and I loved her. So much of her was woven into the fabric of my life, and for several years afterward I kept thinking I should pick up the phone and call her. I did write a song…

Song #36—*Fly Away*

I wasn't going to go back for the funeral because I was absolutely exhausted and didn't know whether I could actually handle it. Thank God for my therapist, Jane. She said she thought I would regret it for the rest of my life. She was right and I did go back.

In the motel the night before the funeral, I was alone in my room, feeling desolate and inconsolable. I prayed for some comfort, and within seconds I felt this rush of energy go through me and had a vision of Sally as a child holding me as a child, and I knew that she was still there in some form—although I still had to grieve the loss. I sang *Fly Away* at her funeral and managed to get through the whole thing without losing it. Once I sat down, the dams burst; and while my other sister, Barbara, was singing the *Lord's Prayer*, I did lose it. Actually, I really wanted to scream. But I'm much too much of a WASP for such public displays. Sally was buried in Winston-Salem, North Carolina, and I've never been back there since.

I went home and cried for many months—for the loss of my sister, for the loss of my home which I had loved so much, for leaving Tahoe and all my friends of the past 18 years, for so many losses. They were mounting up again, and it was hard to deal with it all at once. Puck used to come up to me and put her paws on my shoulders as if she was comforting me. A couple of times, I asked the Universe (actually the angels) for a sign that Sally was okay. One time, within a few hours of that request, three different people brought me sunflowers. I had been sending Sally sunflowers every week for a few months before she died. I guess somebody, somewhere, was actually listening to me.

It's funny how the whole time period from when Sally first was diagnosed, to her death and funeral, is all sort of a blur. I had the same kind of experience when Mummy died. A few things stick out in my mind, but mostly it felt like I was in some kind of zone. I guess that's the way the mind protects itself from the full onslaught of what it means to lose a mother, or a sister, or a friend. I went through many emotions that first year after her death. I was 'pissed' at her again for having lived with my ex-husband, for being unavailable because she was drinking, for all the usual sister stuff from growing up, but mostly for dying before we had the chance to talk about it all.

Five years have gone by, at the writing of this book, and I still miss her. Even though I know she's in another realm and I can actually feel her sometimes, I still feel like I'm hanging onto her in some ways. I have experienced a curious kind of survivor's guilt as well. I think when you're raised in an abusive environment together, it's a bit like being a war veteran or a survivor of a concentration camp. When one of you doesn't make it, the surviving ones have a hard time going on and living a normal life.

Even though I know intellectually that there was nothing I could have done to protect Sally when we were young, or anything I could do to keep her from dying, there is still a part of me that wishes I could have done more. I think my father was more abusive to her than any of us; but he managed to cause almost irreparable harm to all of us. If he were alive, I would sue him...or maybe worse.

The summer after she died, we all met off the coast of North Carolina for a reunion. It was bitter and sweet. I loved being with my whole family all at once and to have all the generations hanging out together. But it was hard to believe that Sally wasn't around anymore. Looking back on it, I think much of my grief was more about our lives than her death. None of us seemed to have escaped the family curse; and Sally, especially, was a major casualty.

That year was also the year of 9/11. Stephanie woke me at 7:00 in the morning and told me to turn on the television. I, along with millions of people all over the world, watched, horrified, as the World Trade Center Towers went down. I was on the other side of the country, but it felt like it was in my own town. I grew up in New York, so it felt very personal. My other sister and her daughter were still living there but were safe. As with most things that I can't do much about, I wrote a song...

Song #37—*Arms Around America*

I sent a CD of the song to President George Bush (who I did NOT vote for) and actually got a formal reply from the

EVIE THOMPSON (EVIE T.)

White House, on pretty fancy, Oval Office stationery. Somehow, I don't think he listened to it, but it felt good to send it.

I was so traumatized already from the past year, that this event really started to send me on a downward spiral, physically and otherwise.

CHAPTER TEN
Kicked out of Eden (Again)

I started playing at a local church (which name I shall not mention, to protect the guilty) during this period, and I felt like it was the only piece of stability I had in my life. I was still relatively new to the area and didn't have a whole lot of support, so the church became my refuge and support. I made new friends and loved playing there. On Mother's Day 2002, all that changed. I decided I would share a new song I had written called *Mary, Tell Me*. I had a 'blast' writing, recording, and then singing it, so I was in my bliss. That day when I finished, I remembered thinking how much I loved being a part of this church. So many people seemed to love me and appreciated all of my musical gifts. Quite a few people came up to me after I sang the song and said how much they liked my voice and the song.

I went to Florida to sing a song I had written for my friends' (Kathy and Steve) wedding. When I returned, the minister of the church said he wanted to have tea with me (uh, oh). He said that he and the Board decided they didn't want me to sing anymore. I asked why. He hemmed and hawed and finally managed to spit out that he didn't like my voice (I knew it was the song). I started crying and asked, "Why not?" The reply was, "Well, it's different." Hmmm… At this point, I could not hold the tears back.

This was the last straw. They wanted me to stay and play the piano but not sing. In other words, stay in the corner and shut up—yet another gag order in my life. I chose to leave rather than be shut up, but it was very painful. Most of the people in the church had no idea what had happened to me or why I left. I felt betrayed personally, professionally, spiritually, and was desperately sad. Perhaps if I hadn't been through so much the year before, I wouldn't have taken the whole incident so personally; but I was in a vulnerable state anyway. The minister did make it into a personal assault, and in my opinion, handled it badly and appallingly unkindly. Ever since then, it has been harder for me to sing in public—yet another blow and abuse of power from a ruling, patriarchal figure.

This was the offending song:
Song #38—*Mary, Tell Me*

For some odd reason, I decided I was going to move from Nevada City to Rough and Ready (out in the boonies) in the middle of all this. I think it had to do with being less expensive, but it didn't turn out to be that way because I ended up having to pay movers twice in a year.

By this time, my health was going downhill. My spine had started folding forward and was pushing on my lungs, stomach and other internal organs. I lost a great deal of weight that I still haven't gained back. I had a year-long anxiety attack which the doctors tried to cure with Atavan. I got addicted to ¼ pill of Atavan a day (which probably wouldn't put a canary to sleep, but it whacked me out) for about a year. Finally, I had to stop taking it because it made me depressed.

One year later, I moved back to the same house I had

moved out of in Nevada City—still in the midst of the longest anxiety attack I've ever had.

I did stay in the women's group in the church. Most of my friends here are from that group, so it was worth my going through the discomfort of remaining anywhere near this minister and his Board. I have since played and sang (nothing controversial!) there a few times (mostly unpaid, I might add) and gone through their chaplain's program. I am now a music chaplain. I have never received an apology, and to this day very few people know what actually happened. I have since found out from someone in the know that it was the song. I have to say, I think I've had it with churches.

The only good thing from this experience was it precipitated my first in-depth, women's lib exploration and search for the Divine Feminine. (I was too busy being a hippy and single parent in the 1960s and 1970s when everyone else was going through it). It made me aware of the hold that patriarchal thinking has not only on our religions but also subliminally on our lives as well.

That year, I wrote and recorded an album dedicated to women's issues called *For All the Women*—my favorite, to date. It is also the most likely album so far to make certain types of people uncomfortable or 'piss' them off. I deal with some pretty heavy-duty issues and raise some interesting questions. I lo----ove it! So there. God has given me a gift for speaking/singing my mind and calling things "as I see's them." Unfortunately, She forgot to give me the requisite armor to withstand the flack after I do.

It took me a long time to process through all that had happened over the past few years. My health took a dive, and I spent almost two years going to doctors and alternative health practitioners trying to figure out exactly what was going on.

Part of the problem was a congenital thing called pectus excavatum (collapsed chest/folding forward of the spine) that still causes me almost constant pain. I also had lung damage and some osteoporosis. I must say, the doctors have not been especially helpful and I've been forced to find other ways of healing myself. I have been slowly getting stronger, but I still have to watch my expenditure of energy.

In October 2004, my daughter's husband left, and another part of my nice, safe, and secure world fell apart. It triggered all of the issues about my parent's divorces and my own. I was deeply affected by the split. I think I was more upset than Stephanie—mostly because she had been unhappy (unbeknownst to me) for a long time. All my holidays and birthdays for the past ten years had been tied up with Derrek's family, and he was like another son to me. Everything suddenly became way more complicated.

It is sad to watch one of your children go through some of the same difficulties you did. I didn't realize during my own divorces just how much everyone is affected—including in-laws, etc. Which doesn't mean divorce is necessarily a bad thing, but the emotional impact can often be underestimated.

I had written a song that I sang at Stephanie and Derrek's wedding that expressed my hopes for their lives together. It was aptly named...

Song #39—*Life Moves On*

It seemed like all hell was breaking loose around the world that year, too. The tsunami in Asia happened the day after Christmas 2004. I can't remember exactly when President Bush decided to invade Iraq, but I do remember he originally pledged some ridiculously low amount of aid (in the low millions) for the survivors of the tsunami, at the same time he allocated some ridiculously high amount (in the billions) for the war in Iraq. Something in me snapped one night while watching back-to-back broadcasts about the unfortunate priorities of our government, and as usual I had to write a song because it caused me so much pain.

<u>Song #40—*Dear Mr. Bush*</u>

I have yet to send it to him.

I was getting ready to record this song with my vocal coach, Reinhardt. We had a date set to go into the studio, but the date came and went, and I never heard from him. I left him several messages over the next few weeks, but no response. I had a friend do a tarot reading for me that indicated there was going to be a huge amount of chaos related to a younger man who was having financial problems. I would find out the significance of this in about a week. I kept getting more and more 'wigged out' about it, so I finally called his teacher, Seth Riggs, in Los Angeles. Seth told me Reinhardt had committed suicide on the day before we were supposed to record. (I almost took it personally). I knew he was having financial problems and apparently had developed a drug problem as well. I was so sad about this. He was such a lovely, talented, sensitive person (and he loved my song!). He reminded me of my brother-in-law, Luis, who was also gay and committed suicide. Here was yet another piece of my safe little world falling away.

A couple of months after this, my beloved dog, Puck, was diagnosed with a cancerous tumor in her hip. The only way to excise the tumor would be to cut off her leg. I knew I couldn't do that to her or me, so I took her home and prepared for her to die in the next couple of months. I went through major grieving and wrote this song (actually she wrote it through me—to me. Move over Shirley MacLaine!).

Song #41—*I'll Be There*

I'm happy to say that as of today, almost one year later, Puck is still with me. She proved three veterinarians wrong. I think she knows I'm not ready for her to go yet. Probably, I never will be; but for now, I am grateful for every day I have left with her.

CHAPTER ELEVEN
And She Lived Happily Ever After...

I had an interesting dream during the course of writing this book. In the dream, a higher being was unplugging a cord that was going from me to the external world and plugging it back into me. The cord represented my life-long tendency to cast about outside myself looking for something that would save me from the circumstances of my life and allow me to live somebody else's life—anybody's life—other than my own. When the cord got plugged back into me at the core of my being, I felt a surge of the most overwhelming pain along with the sweetest feeling of completeness coming from living in the flow of my own life-stream. It loses a little in the translation from dream life to waking life, but it was a psyche-altering dream, and I still feel the effects of it.

I'm embarrassed to admit that every time I went to type "Riches to Rags" during the writing of this book, I ended up typing "Riches to Rage"—ostensibly because "s" and "e" are only one finger apart on the keyboard. I think it's probably more of a Freudian-finger-slip, however.

It's always been much easier for me to muster up outrage for other people's issues. I get absolutely incensed about the abuse of women, children, and animals, and have been a vociferous defender of the underdogs and downtrodden of the world. I have spoken up for, cried for, and acted on behalf of other women, other children, the Earth, animals, sometimes even for men. But I have rarely been able to speak up for, cry for, or act on behalf of myself. I still have a hard time directly accessing and externalizing my feelings of outrage about what happened to me and end up beating myself up instead.

The deeper I go into my own issues and feelings, the more I seem to touch on universal themes. The devastation wrought by the patriarchal system in my own family is but one more individual story in a long line of stories going back to Adam and Eve, or to whenever one-half of the human race decided it was superior to the other half. All of our religions and institutions are riddled with this patriarchal sickness, and it affects all of us—men and women—on a level so profound it is almost inaccessible to the conscious mind. Show me a patriarchal system of any kind, and I'll show you the rape and abuse of women and children, the subjugation of entire cultures, unending wars and terrorism, decimation of other species, destruction of our planet, and a disconnection from the web of life that is so vast that it boggles the mind and breaks our collective heart.

I grew up in a family, and we live in a society that dishonors feelings to such an extent that most people will do anything not to feel their own pain. So many of us turn to alcohol, drugs, cigarettes (alas, my current personal and politically-incorrect favorite), food, anti-depressants, workaholism, pornography, religious obsession, and a whole list of other distractions and busyness, that we are totally incapable of tuning into what is actually going on in our lives.

People who cannot deal with their own pain have a tendency to inflict that pain on others in some form or another. People who don't feel what they're really feeling are generally easily manipulated by outside authority figures and don't speak up about outrageous abuses because they have become anesthetized to their own, or anyone else's pain.

There are things going on in this world that require our outrage or they will never change. We should be outraged when another woman or child falls prey to yet another predator. We should be outraged when women in Africa or India are still being genitally mutilated. We should be outraged when our politicians blatantly and pathologically lie to us to pad their own pockets. We should be mad as hell when our old people are being cast aside and abused by their own caretakers, when they should be honored and revered. We should all stand up and scream, "We're mad as hell, and we're not going to take it anymore!" (to borrow from the movie *Network*). Silence is, in the end, complicity.

We all need to feel the depth of our own individual pain so that we can cease to project it outwards. It is not enough to say it's the human condition and that's the way it has always been. Just because that's the way it has always been (which is disputable anyway) doesn't mean that that's the way it should be. Part of the human condition is feeling our feelings; and if we cease to have them, we cease to be human. For some reason we have spawned generations of Spocks, and it is killing us all. When I was meditating one day, I heard a Voice say this: "It is more important to be human than it is to be more than human." I believe it is by fully embracing our humanity—in all its joys and sorrows and all its tragedies and triumphs—that we, at last, touch our own divinity.

There is a scene in a movie called *Powder* that pretty much sums up my feelings on this subject. There is a macho, hunter-type guy and his cronies standing around a deer they have just shot. The deer is still alive, and the man who shot him is telling the younger men in his group that the deer doesn't feel any pain. Powder grabs the guy's hand and places it on the deer and somehow manages to transmit the deer's pain to the guy.

The guy looks like he's being electrocuted as the overwhelming pain of the deer shoots through him. Needless to say, the guy was terrified of and hated Powder for it, but apparently he never picked up a gun or shot another deer again.

Curiously, my billionaire cousin (who likes to pretend our side of the family doesn't exist) produced this movie. Even more curiously, our family (my parents, his parents, and our grandparents) loved to shoot living creatures for amusement. It was considered great sport to shoot little birds, chase foxes with a pack of dogs, or pay huge sums of money to go on safari in Africa for more exotic kills. I, personally, have always hated guns. I'm not sure of my cousin's feelings about all this, but I sure liked his movie.

I now know that the people who inflicted their pain on me were in a great deal of pain themselves. I also know that when I didn't or couldn't feel my own pain, I often unconsciously inflicted it on those I loved the most, and for that I am truly sorry.

I wish I could say that I am now totally enlightened, that I now have all the answers, and that I never have a day where I run from my own feelings and pain in one way or another. I wish I could say that I am now blissfully happy all the time, that I never revert back to being two years old again, and that, because I have felt so much of my own pain, I will never cause anyone else pain again. I wish I could say all that.

But the truth is, I'm only human. I frequently get thrown back into terrifying flashbacks and body memories, but at least now, I know where they're coming from. I still don't like baths because of my association with molestation, so I let myself take showers instead. I still have trouble allowing myself to have the full range of my feelings, although I am instantly aware of what I'm doing. I am definitely NOT blissfully happy all the time, but there is an underlying contentment to my days. I still have a tendency to want to stick my head in the sand and not speak up for myself or go to the other extreme and blast the first person who crosses my path—but I do much less of both. I am still prone to catastrophic thinking because so much of my life WAS catastrophic. But I am now capable of decatastrophizing (is that a word?) fairly rapidly. I still have trouble staying in my body, but I am generally more comfortable in my own skin and actually enjoy my own company.

In terms of the title *Riches to Rags (and back again)*, I must say I think I went a little bit overboard in an effort to disinherit my inheritance and have gotten a little too close to the 'Rags' for my own comfort. I buy most of my clothes at thrift shops (thus, the rags); and the last few years, I have not always had enough to cover the essentials (like rent, health insurance, etc.) without running up my credit card. So—(to the Powers that Be), give it back! (just kidding—sort of). I often think of one of the last scenes in the movie *Arthur*. Dudley Moore (Arthur) has given up all of his fortune for the woman he loves, but somehow his grandmother ends up giving it to him anyway. He says something to the effect of, "I'm not stupid, you know." Meaning, maybe he could have his cake and eat it, too. Bingo. Maybe I can, too!

The trouble with being born rich is that you've already had everything everyone else spends their whole lives running after, so there is nowhere to go but down or in. I did a lot of both. I have been, simultaneously, greatly blessed and greatly cursed. I am not sure, karmically speaking, what the point of it all has been, but I do know that my only job is to make something out of what I have been given (good or bad). I think I have done that. Rest assured, though, that I intend to give the Higher-Ups a piece of my mind when this particular incarnation is over.

I'm a little scared to end this book. I think there's been a suspicion lurking in the back of my mind that if I wrote the story of my life, when the book ended, my life would end. What I'm really hoping is that the end of this book marks the beginning of the rest of my life, and that the past can now dwell in the past, so that I can live without shackles. To tell you the truth, I almost cannot even imagine what it would be like to live free, but I'm sure going to give it a try.

Song #42—*I'm Gonna Go out Singin'*
Song #43—*Riches to Rags (and back again)*

DEDICATION

For All the Women…

<u>Song #44—*For All the Women*</u>

and for all the men who were born of wo-men--
may we all be free

The music and lyrics for all the songs in this book were written and recorded by Evie Thompson, aka Evie T. The songs can be found on the following CDs:

KEEPING ME COMPANY
You've Got it All
Longing to be Free
Don't Cry in the Morning
Breakdown
Out of my Mind
Angels Don't Sleep
Other Side of Night
Is That Too Much to Ask
Puppet on a String

WINGS OF CHANGE
You Lift Me Up
Life Moves On
Wings of Change
She Will Stand
Metamorphosis
Lovers on the Lam
Rivers Run Red
You Can Stay
WASP Blues
Take Me to the Edge
You're Not the Cure
Standing in a Circle of Love

WALK INTO THE WIND
Walk Into the Wind
I've Got a Hit Song
Heartland

EVIE THOMPSON (EVIE T.)

Freefall
Children of the Sun
In My Father's House
Love Looking at Me
Hotline to Heaven
Angel's Gift
If I'm Good Enough for God
Fascist Swing
Christmas

A HIGHER PLACE

A Higher Place
Who are We?
The Indian Way
No Goodbyes
Call of the Wild
Hard to Believe
Where the Songs Come From
Dancing on the Wind
A Little Child Shall Lead Us
Shadowboxing
Lady of the Stars
Breaking Out

THERE'S A HAND

There's a Hand
Shalom
Voyagers to Love
Fast Track to Glory
Grace
The Better it Gets
Mother of All
Heaven is My Zipcode
Now That Jesus is My Friend

For Enlightenment
The Sinners and the Saints
God is God

DOORS AND WINDOWS

Even Here
Mister Anxiety
Unsung Heroes
One Woman, One Man
Someone Who Moves Me
The UnSong
If This Were My Last Day
Move the Rock
Open Up My Doors and Windows
Soul For Sale
Angels Before Me
Walk on the Water
Secrets & Lies

ALL THE LIGHTS IN HOLLYWOOD

Arms Around America
I'm Gonna Go Out Singin'
Ticket Outta Here
One People
All the Lights in Hollywood
You Can Count on Me
Stand With Me
Walk Right Here
Fly Away
Light Up the Stars
Hurry Home

EVIE THOMPSON (EVIE T.)

<u>FOR ALL THE WOMEN</u>
For All the Women
Mary, Tell Me
What if Every Little Girl
Whose Body is This, Anyway?
Pray for This Woman
Dancing in Eden
You Go, Girl
Secrets & Lies
Mother, Where Were You?
Touch Me with Love
She Will Stand
Mother of All

Not all the songs on these CDs are in the book. If you are interested in the others, they are available from:

Amazon.com (type Evie T. into "search")
CDBaby.com (type Evie T. into "search")

Or write to:
EVT RECORDS
P.O. Box 1794
Nevada City, CA 95959

All songs are copywritten by the US Copyright Office and are registered with ASCAP.

All the above CDs (with the exception of *Keeping Me Company* which was recorded at Studio D in Sausalito, CA) were recorded at Moonlight Studios in Los Angeles and were co-produced and arranged with David Vasquez. Programming and keyboards also by David Vasquez.

APPENDIX
(Song Lyrics)

SONG #1
Lady of the Stars

The winged ones told me when I was born
      seven stars danced round my head
      not a crown of thorns
and on my heart strings angels played
      melodies of long ago and very far away
another star in the dark skies
another child with God in the eyes
oooooooh oooooooh

LADY OF THE STARS COMIN' DOWN
      TO SHINE
LADY OF THE STARS BACK TO CLAIM
      WHAT'S MINE
LADY OF THE STARS MAGNETIZIN'
      LIGHTNIN'
LADY OF THE STARS CHASE AWAY WHAT'S
      FRIGHTENIN'
LADY OF THE STARS, BRINGER OF THE
      DAWN
LADY OF THE STARS, BRINGER OF THE
      DAWN

Sliding down on a starstream I weaved my way
      lured by the kiss of dreams
      to build a brand new day.

The sounds of heaven kept haunting me,
 calling forth the unseen world
 for everyone to see.
Trailing spirals of stardust
 blazing pathways and learning to trust.

oooooooooh oooooooooh

CHORUS

I'll whistle and I'll sing til the walls of
 Jericho come down.
Climb Jacob's ladder till I'm free.
Make a joyful noise so they'll know that I'm around
 and frolic in Gethsemane.

CHORUS

© 1996 Evie Thompson

SONG #2
Secrets and Lies

He called it playin' doctor 'cause he had an MD,
    but something in me knew he wasn't healing me.
I rolled right up in a fetal ball at the end of my bed,
    held my breath, closed my eyes so he'd think
    I was dead.
Waitin' for his footsteps and the sound of my name,
    I turned to stone and built the walls for
    a houseful of shame.

SECRETS, SECRETS AND LIES
SILENCE RULES OR SOMEBODY DIES
SECRETS, SECRETS AND LIES
DON'T SEEM TO MATTER WHEN A LITTLE GIRL
CRIES, SECRETS

He smelled of booze and cigarettes,
    had hands that were too thick.
Used a scarf to shut me up,
    said Mommy was too sick.
Said I was a whore and that I'd surely go to hell.
Said "that ain't rape, it's just love,
    so make sure you never tell."

EVIE THOMPSON (EVIE T.)

CHORUS

The sins of the father stop right here;
  whoa, no more wearin' of another man's fear.

CHORUS

SONG #3
What if Every Little Girl

I know of a little girl from India,
    thrown on the side of a road.
Left cause she had the wrong genitalia.
Supposedly, karma she had sowed.
And I know how she feels,
    even in America,
      what it's like not to matter very much.

WHAT IF EVERY LITTLE GIRL CAME INTO
THIS LIFE A TREASURE? WHAT IF EVERY
LITTLE GIRL KNEW HER FACE WOULD
GIVE GOD PLEASURE? WHAT IF EVERY
LITTLE GIRL COULD LOOK FORWARD TO
TOMORROW? WHAT IF EVERY LITTLE GIRL
COULD RISE ABOVE HER SORROW?

Who will look back at her from the mirror
    if no one believes in her soul?
Why would she talk if you don't hear her
    or honor the magic that she holds?
Even one little girl could change all the world
    if she knew that she mattered very much
CHORUS
And will you stand up for her
    so she knows you are there?

And will you really listen
    so she knows that you care?
Will you be her hero
    til she sees herself reflected in your eye
CHORUS

© 2003 Evie Thompson

SONG #4
Mother, Where Were You?

Mother, where were you when darkness fell
    and my bed became my tomb?
Mother, where were you when Daddy raised hell
    and crept into my room?
Were you there and did you hear my cryin'
    in the middle of the night?
Were you there when your little girl was dyin'
    for you to make it all right?

Mother, where were you when I had nowhere to turn
    but to drugs and alcohol?
Mother, where were you when I was losin' my mind
    and wanted to end it all?
Did you know how much I needed you to be there
    so I could make it through?
Did you know that when I got older
    I'd still be missin' you?

Mother, where were you when I rode in that car
    with boys who didn't care?
Mother, where were you when the hospital called
    and said that I was there?
Where were you when I began to be a woman
    but didn't quite know how?

EVIE THOMPSON (EVIE T.)

How could you die just when I found you,
    can you hear me now?

I'm always with you, you're never alone,
I'm always by your side.

I always loved you, it may not have shown,
    but God knows how hard I tried.
I'll be there and if you ever need me,
    just call my name somehow.
I'll be there and I will never leave
    —can you feel me now?
Can you hear me now? Can you hear me now?

© 2002 Evie Thompson

SONG #5
W.A.S.P. Blues

Well, my mama she was a smooth aristocrat
    and my daddy he didn't know where it's at.
Don't feel, don't be real.
I got the white Anglo Saxon Protestant blues.

Well, I lived on Park Avenue
    and I couldn't do what I wanted to do.
Be cool, don't break the rules.
I got the white Anglo Saxon Protestant blues.

I got the blues—the low down, upper East Side blues.
Well, uptight, I got the blues 'most every night.
But my heart keeps on a singin'
    and my head keeps on a ringin'.
I got the white Anglo Saxon Protestant blues.

I got the blues, reluctant debutante blues.
I got the blues, I-never-got-to-be-me blues.
Kinda wish I'd been born in Harlem
    'cause my soul keeps callin' darlin'.
Gotta sing the blues.

I got the white Anglo, etc.

© 1991 Evie Thompson

SONG #6
A Little Child Shall Lead Us

Somewhere at midnight,
 on the darkened streets of hell,
There's a child that keeps walkin'.
And somewhere out of sight, a child who'd rather die
 than tell keeps on talkin'.
And if you're very quiet, you can hear a song,
 a tiny voice—a spirit—that don't belong
 to this world as it is.
It's a cold hard place,
 but nothing can stop a child named Grace.

AND A LITTLE CHILD SHALL LEAD US
 FROM THE DARKNESS TO THE LIGHT.
A LITTLE CHILD SHALL LEAD US
 UNTIL WE ALL SHINE BRIGHT.
WHOA—A LITTLE CHILD SHALL LEAD US.
 A LITTLE CHILD SHALL FREE US.
A LITTLE CHILD SHALL TAKE OUR HANDS
 AND THEN WE'LL GO HOME AGAIN.

Somewhere all alone on a trail of false desires,
 there's a child that keeps cryin'.
And somewhere far from home,
 a stranger in a strange land keeps on tryin'

And every time a tear falls
    or a heart breaks wide,
A little love comes closer
    to the fear inside.

Then peace rushes in, time holds still.
    The sun burns off the nighttime chill.

CHORUS

Ooooooooo—a little closer now
Ooooooooo—hush
Ooooooooo—can you feel it now?
Ooooooooo

CHORUS

© 1996 Evie Thompson

SONG #7
God Don't Make No Junk

If someone says you're stupid;
    well that don't make it so.
Just because you're different
    from what other people know,
    don't mean you're not just the way you're
    supposed to be.
Who knows what you'll do one day
    if only you believe.

GOD DON'T MAKE NO JUNK
    NOBODY'S A MISTAKE.
GOD DON'T MAKE NO JUNK,
    BE YOU, FOR HEAVEN'S SAKE.
GOD DON'T MAKE NO JUNK,
    DON'T MAKE NO JUNK,
    DON'T MAKE NO JUNK. NO JUNK.
GOD DON'T MAKE NO JUNK,
    DON'T MAKE NO JUNK,
    DON'T MAKE NO JUNK. NO JUNK.

Imagine you're surrounded by a
    multi-colored shield
    that keeps you safe and bounces off
    the sticks and stones you feel.
Stand your ground and know that you

can look them in the eye.
Keep your chin up and be proud;
you're a star in God's own sky.

CHORUS

...show the people who you are
...love yourself and you'll go far

CHORUS

© 2005 Evie Thompson

SONG #8
If I'm Good Enough for God

Maybe I'm not tall. Maybe I don't play the
    saxophone.
Maybe I can't do it all. Maybe I don't quite fit the
    mold.
But I know that I was meant to be
    just exactly who I am today;
    and I know if I could only see
    with the eyes of God, I'd be ok.

IF I'M GOOD ENOUGH FOR GOD,
    I AM GOOD ENOUGH FOR ME.
IF I'M GOOD ENOUGH FOR GOD,
    I AM ALL THAT I CAN BE.
IF I'M GOOD ENOUGH FOR GOD,
    THEN I'M GOOD ENOUGH FOR NOW.
IF I'M GOOD ENOUGH FOR GOD,
    THEN I GUESS I AM ALLOWED TO BE ME.

Maybe I'm not perfect,
    maybe I'm not all the world expected.
Maybe I haven't made it yet,
    maybe I don't do as directed.
But I know there's no one quite like me,
    no one who can walk inside my shoes.
And I know if I could hear God's voice,

I'd hear, "My child, I'm proud of you."

CHORUS

I can't believe in something that can't believe in me.
And I can't live with someone else's
    second-hand decree.
I've looked the whole world over,
    for something that is mine.
Now I'm right back where I started from,
    and this time I'm not blind.

CHORUS

© 1995 Evie Thompson

SONG #9
Ticket Outta Here

When I'd wake in the middle of the night,
    reach for somethin' just to stop the pain,
I'd take the cork from the bottle and feel all right,
    seemed to soothe my troubled brain.
And if that didn't work, I'd pop a pill,
    eat Haagen-Dazs 'til I got ill.
And if that didn't work, I had a better idea,
    If all else fails, I'll get me a man
    (yeah, that's the ticket).

TICKET, TICKET, TICKET OUTTA HERE.
IF THE FRYIN' PAN'S HOT,
    I'LL JUMP IN THE FIRE.
TICKET, TICKET, TICKET OUTTA HERE.
    BEAM ME UP BEFORE I EXPIRE.
I NEED MY TICKET OUTTA HERE.
GIMME MY TICKET OUTTA HERE.
THERE MUST BE A WAY OUTTA HERE.
GIMME MY TICKET OUTTA HERE.

No relief when I shopped 'til I dropped.
No religion gave me my reward.
Even geographics didn't work 'til I stopped
    and realized I was bored
    with all the drama inside my own head

fightin' with legions of the dead.
You'd think I'd learn,
    but it's part of the fun.
Aw, hell, I'll get me another one (man, that is).

CHORUS

And if I had a whole pile o' money,
I'd buy my way into the land o' milk and honey,
With my

CHORUS

© 2002 Evie Thompson

SONG #10
Soul For Sale

Waitin' for her pimp to come,
    the sidewalk girl grows cold.
Hidin' in a bottle of rum,
    lookin' for the life she sold.
Dancin' in fear on an asphalt stage,
    sways to the siren's wail,
    prisoner of a gogo cage.
    Spends her nights in jail, singin'...

SOUL FOR SALE,
    THE BIDDING HAS BEGUN.
SOUL FOR SALE,
    THE LADY'S COME UNDONE.
GOIN' ONCE, GOIN, TWICE,
    GONE FOR THE LOWEST PRICE.
SOUL FOR SALE.

Hidin' on Park Avenue, the socialite plays games.
Waitin' for her broker
    to bring drugs with legal names.
Trades her body for a wedding ring,
    lives in a gilded cage.
Still believes in the Cinderella thing,
    forgets to come of age, singin'...

CHORUS
Look in the mirror, what do you see?
Looks a bit like you and me, singin'...
CHORUS

© 1999 Evie Thompson

SONG #11
Freefall

In the middle of the night,
When I reach for you and desire floods my soul.
I wanna hold you tight—
     have a good time, to touch you everywhere 'til
     you lose control.
Well, I won't hold back anything,
     'cause I wanna turn you on.
I wanna hear you whisperin'
     that you wanna make love to me all night long.

FREEFALL, FREEFALL,
     INTO THE ARMS OF LOVE.
FREEFALL, FREEFALL,
     WELL, CATCH ME, CATCH ME.

Let's take our time,
     make every minute count.
Throw ourselves into the rivers of fire,
     celebrate the night.
Let our passions out,
     set our hearts to dancin' until the sunrise.
Give ourselves over to the rhythm of romance,
     that is pumpin' through our veins.
Let's jump right in, take the chance,
lay aside our fears and try it again.

CHORUS

ooooooooooooooooooooh ooooh I love you darlin'

ooooooooooooooooooooh ooooh I'm fallin'

CHORUS

© 1995 Evie Thompson

SONG #12
Unsung Heroes

We may never see them in the magazines
    and we may even be them,
    the ones with invisible dreams.
But anyone who's raised a child
    or buried their best friend,
    faced the night without a drink, with no
    awards at the end.

SO I SING FOR THE UNSUNG HEROES,
    THE ANONYMOUS ARMY.
AND I BOW TO THE UNSUNG HEROES
    AND THEY LOOK LIKE YOU AND ME.

They might walk unnoted in our neighborhood;
    And they may not be quoted or be understood.
But anyone who keeps on standing when all around
    them fall,
Deserves a purple heart for life, deserves to have it
    all.

CHORUS

Ordinary superstars,
    living valiantly.

Enduring all the battle scars,
    to be free.

CHORUS

© 1998 Evie Thompson

SONG #13
You're Not the Cure

You never took any time to get to know me,
    And you didn't care.
You didn't listen to a word I said,
    Just to show me that you wouldn't care.

I tried so hard to reach your heart,
    But you closed off again.
Another time you put me down,
    And now you've lost a friend.

YOU'RE NOT THE CURE, BABY,
    YOU'RE THE PAIN.
YOU DROVE ME CRAZY,
GOT ME ALL MESSED UP,
TOLD ME SO MANY LIES,
YOU WANTED TO TRY AND BREAK ME.
BUT I WALKED THE OTHER WAY.
YOU'RE NOT THE CURE, BABY,
    YOU'RE THE PAIN, etc.

You always took this love of mine so lightly,
    made me wanna cry.
You only wanted me when it suited you,
    it's not likely that I'll wanna try.

The only thing that mattered was
    what was good for you.
You wouldn't see I had a life,
I had to say you're not my friend.

CHORUS

You couldn't give,
    I couldn't live
    with nothin' in return.
I won't carry your load,
    baby gonna hit the road
    and follow my own dream.

CHORUS

© 1993 Evie Thompson

SONG #14
Even Here

I think it's pretty easy,
    to see God in the flowers.
To keep the faith when I'm ridin' high,
    in my finest hours.
But it ain't so easy when I'm walkin' thru the valley
    and the shadow of death has me cornered
    in an alley.
Gotta remember then

EVEN HERE, EVEN NOW,
    GOD IS IN THIS PLACE.
EVEN HERE, EVEN NOW,
    THE RIVER OF HIS GRACE FLOWS.
EVEN HERE, EVEN NOW.

Sometimes it feels like I'm nobody
    with nowhere to go.
Missin' whatever it takes
    to get on with the show.
And it's hard to feel rich when you ain't got no
    money,
And it's hard to imagine the land of milk and honey
    when you're in hell, but

CHORUS
When I can't go on walking'
And I can't stand anymore,
Then you carry me...
CHORUS

SONG #15
No Goodbyes

Mummy, Daddy, Peter and Luis.
Bunny and Diego, Grandma Boggs and Grandpa
Lamb.
Uncle Marshie, Grandpa Field, Anne Clouet, Anne
Beth.
Are you all together now and can you tell me how;
     how to keep on loving and keep on losing and
     keep on loving again.
How to keep on giving and keep on living and keep
     on being a friend.

Evie, we are standing right beside you now.
Hello from Heaven,
     we're watching over you (don't doubt).
Just say hello.

NO GOODBYES. NO FAREWELLS.
     EVERYONE IS COMING HOME.
RING THE BELLS 'CAUSE NO ONE'S EVER
     LEFT ALONE.
NO ONE'S TEARS WILL GO UNKNOWN.
NO GOODBYES, WE ARE HERE.
     NO GOODBYES, HAVE NO FEAR.
NO GOODBYES.

Lisa, Coors, Darcy and John.
Dr. D and Anastasia, Jean Clouet and Dot.
John Lennon, Martin, Robert and Jack.
I've lit your candles in my heart
     and your names will carry me far.

And I'll keep on trying and keep on crying
     and keep on doing my best.
I'll keep on believing and keep on achieving
     and keep on in my quest.

Evie, you are standing on a threshold now,
     a whole new way of living.
All of us are part of you (don't doubt).
Just say hello.

CHORUS

Crossing the bridges of time and space,
     our love moves you into your place.
We will move heaven and earth for your grace.
Just say hello.

CHORUS (twice)

© 1996 Evie Thompson

SONG #16
Puppet on a String

Giving you up is so hard to do.
> kickin' the habit is drivin' me wild.

Wastin' my time tryin' to get you to love me,
> breakin' my heart tryin' to make you aware
> that I have feelings, too.

Oh, listen to me—you're afraid to even try.

The writin's on the wall
> and every stranger on the street
> looks and talks like you.

HEY, LOOK AT ME NOW.
I'M A PUPPET ON A STRING
HANGIN' ON YOUR EVERY WORD
AND WISHIN' I WAS FREE.

Takin' it easy is takin' its toll.
> Walkin' around it, it never gets solved.

I'm standing alone when you say that you're with me
> pretendin' I'm strong when I want you to know
> that I have feelings, too.

Oh, listen to me—you're afraid to even try.
> The writin's on the wall

and every stranger on the street
looks and talks like you.

CHORUS

© 1990 Evie Thompson

SONG #17
Angels Don't Sleep

Whatever you say, whatever you do,
    I'll be there for you.
And when it comes down to takin' the vows
    I'll be true to you,
'Cause I fell in love with your angel
    watchin' you asleep.
I fell in love with the things you hide
    when mornin' comes again.

ANGELS DON'T SLEEP IN THE NIGHTTIME,
    SHADOWS CAN'T COVER YOUR HEART.
ANGELS DON'T SLEEP WHEN YOU CLOSE
    YOUR EYES,
THERE IS NO NEED TO HIDE.

You can't keep me out,
    no matter how hard you try.
I'll be there for you
    and if you are runnin' scared, so am I.
But I'll be true to you
    'cause I fell in love with your angel
    while you were off your guard.

I fell in love with everything,
    you try so hard to deny.

CHORUS.

SONG #18
Now That Jesus is My Friend

For so many years I felt lonely and lost,
   with nowhere to turn, no one to talk to.
The weight of the world was an oppressive cross,
   my life was a game with no meaning or clue.
Now I stand on a precipice, ready to fall,
   and I hear a voice calling my name.
He says, "Come, follow me, I'll take care of it all,
   stand in the SON not the rain."

NOW JESUS IS MY FRIEND,
   I WILL NEVER BE LONELY AGAIN.
NOW THAT JESUS IS MY FRIEND,
   ALL MY MISTAKES HAVE BEEN FORGIVEN.
NOW THAT JESUS IS MY FRIEND,
   I'LL WALK WITH HIM, HAND IN HAND
   TO HEAVEN.
NOW THAT JESUS IS MY FRIEND, etc., etc.

We've been round and round, Jesus and I.
There are days I don't trust him or listen to reason.
Sometimes I get angry and sometimes I cry,
   when he tells me to wait, for everything there's
   a season.
But I know he won't leave me, betray me like most.
His love sees through all of my armor and I can't

comprehend why he holds me so close, without asking me to try harder.

CHORUS

In his eyes, I am a star.
In his heart, I am a sister.
In his Grace, I will go far.
He believes in me.

CHORUS

© 1998 Evie Thompson

SONG #19
Walk on the Water

Just when I think I've gone as far as I can,
    the fisher of men knocks on my door, and says,
"Put down your nets, come follow me—
    stick with me kid, I'm gonna show you more.
I'll take you to places that you've never been,
    reach deep inside you and set you free.
We'll sail through storms to the heart of the
    ocean of eternity."

WALK ON THE WATER, DANCE ON THE AIR.
    LOOK HOW THE BIG BOYS DO IT.
WALK ON THE WATER, TRY IF YOU DARE.
    I'M GONNA WALK YOU RIGHT THROUGH
    IT.

Let your eye be single, see nothing but me.
    Don't let the waves of your fear drag you down.
If I say you can do it, trust in me.
    I'll carry you to shore, I won't let you drown.
I'll save your life if you lay it down for me.
    I'll be your radar when you can't see.
I'll calm the waters
    and we'll ride the winds of mystery.

CHORUS

Father…where are you taking me?
How can I leave behind everything I know
for somewhere I can't see?
Abba…why am I scared to be free?

Why do the chains on my soul
seem sometimes more inviting to me?

CHORUS

© 1998 Evie Thompson

EVIE THOMPSON (EVIE T.)

SONG #20
The Indian Way

While walking in the woods one day,
I met a wise old Indian man.
He talked of signs and the Indian way,
    as a river of tears flowed for his land.
There was a time when buffalos danced
    and forests sang to the sky.
When the voice of Mother Earth still had a chance
    and our ears were tuned to her cries.

LISTEN, LISTEN, LISTEN TO THE WHISPERS
    OF HER CHILDREN.
ALL OF US ARE ONE.
EVERY ROCK AND EVERY CREATURE
    IS SOMEONE.
THIS IS THE INDIAN WAY.
    TREAT SOMEONE THE INDIAN WAY.
SPEAK YOUR HEART.
    THIS IS THE INDIAN WAY.

He looked at me with love in his eyes and said,
"Honor yourself as much as others.
Our nations have clashed—spilled blood and lies,
    but under the skin we are brothers.
There'll come a time when skyscrapers bow
    and mountains rise from the sea,

when the white buffalo walks thru the middle of
town
and the earth claims her majesty."

CHORUS

Walk softly on the earth—leave no footprints behind.
    Remember you are but her shepherd.
Great Spirit is alive—let it guide you from inside
    And do what you can to keep her.

CHORUS

© 1996 Evie Thompson

SONG #21
Children of the Sun

We come in every shape and size,
    every color, every walk of life.
Some of us walk the straight way,
    some of us are gay.
But we all want the same things,
    we are working side by side.
In our hearts we are all queens and kings
    with the power—to make love come alive.

WE ARE MARCHING TO A NEW WORLD.
WE ARE CHILDREN OF THE SUN.
WE ARE SEEDLINGS OF A NEW URGE
    AND WE KNOW THAT WE ARE ONE.
WE ARE SINGING A NEW SONG.
WE ARE CHILDREN OF THE SUN.
WE ARE MILLIONS AND WE STAND STRONG.
WE ARE CHILDREN OF THE SUN.

We live by all different creeds,
    different values, different kinds of needs.
Some of us are women
    and some of us are men.
But we all come from the same place
    and we're all going home.
In our hearts, there is only one human race
    with the power—to grant each other grace.

CHORUS
Someday when our minds start blowin' in the wind,
We will open up our hearts and let each other in.
CHORUS

SONG #22
Call of the Wild

Deep in the forest where the wolves run wild,
    the waters speak my name
    and every blade of grass waves as I go by.
Singin' girl, don't ever get tame.
    You can't own the wind, can't stop the rains, whoa.
    Can't hold a sunbeam in your hand, yeah.
    You can't tie a cloud, can't put a bird in chains.
Listen to the music of the land.

THE CALL OF THE WILD—NATURE'S CHILD.
THE CALL OF THE WILD—COME PLAY A
    WHILE.
THE CALL OF THE WILD IS WAKIN' ME.
THE CALL OF THE WILD IS TAKIN' ME.
THE CALL OF THE WILD IS MAKIN' ME
—WILD.

When the moon is full and the stars all dance,
    the winged ones come for me.
And we spin around the fire in a shaman's trance
    singing' girl, you gotta be free.
You can walk on water,
    you can travel thru time, whoa.
Think a thing and it will come true, yeah.
You can be anything,

you can shape-shift reality.
Listen to the symphony of you.

CHORUS

Getting' down and dirty in the soil of imagination,
    stripping down to soul the heart of all creation.
Ashes to ashes—dust to dust,
    we all go back to the earth's crust.

CHORUS

© 1996 Evie Thompson

SONG #23
The Better it Gets

Some people say if it's too good,
    it's too good to be true.
And other people say if you fly too high,
    you're bound to hit a ceiling if you do.
But I say the sky's the limit,
    there's so much you can do, if you don't hold back.
I say like Newton's law of motion,
    if you got enough momentum you can beat the
lack.

CAUSE THE BETTER IT GETS,
    THE BETTER IT GETS.
A ROLLING STONE KEEPS GATHERING
    SPEED.
THE BETTER IT GETS, THE BETTER IT GETS.
THERE WILL BE AN ANSWER FOR EVERY
    NEED.
THE BETTER IT GETS, THE BETTER IT GETS.
THE BETTER IT GETS, THE BETTER IT GETS.
THE BETTER IT GETS, THE BETTER IT GETS.

You can soar and rise above the Peter Principle.
    'cause every rule has its exception, your spirit
    is invincible.

I say there's a way to play the game,
    where the rich get richer and the poor get rich.
I say where you keep on lookin' will keep on cookin'
    and create what you wish.

CHORUS

Give, and in the giving is the living love of life.
Sing, and in the singing is the gift of flight.

CHORUS

© 1998 Evie Thompson

SONG #24
Voyagers to Love

Love like a river carries us back to the sea
    where our hearts are calling to remember
    the meeting of souls like you and me.
A lifetime of drifting is over now,
    our bodies and spirits are drinking 'til we drown,
And we're moving to waves of ecstasy
    on an uncharted course to somewhere heavenly.

WE ARE VOYAGERS (echo) TO LOVE (echo)
    AND WE GOT PROMISES TO KEEP.
WE ARE VOYAGERS (echo) TO LOVE (echo)
    FEELIN' HIGH AND GOIN' DEEP.
WE ARE VOYAGERS (echo) TO LOVE (echo)
    COAXING EACH OTHER FROM SLEEP.
WE ARE VOYAGERS (echo) TO LOVE (echo)
    WE ARE VOYAGERS TO LOVE.

Out on the ocean with the wind at our backs
    and our arms open wide,
    ready for lovin' and dreamin'
    knowing the fears will soon subside.
Our energies risin, breathin' entwined,
    the struggle is over, our stars are aligned
    and we're sailin' no longer traveling alone,
    the power of love will take us home.

CHORUS

Love is leading us on,
    Dryin' our tears and making us strong.

Thru all the storms across all the years,
    May we always be in love.

CHORUS

© 1997 Evie Thompson

SONG #25
You've Got it All

In the blink of an eye
I watched you grow up from a child
    into a girl with wild hair and fire in your eyes.
I think of all the joys and all of the tears,
    the times we fought,
    the times we faced all our fears.

YOU'RE WALKIN' TALL, NOW, BABY.
YOU MAY FALL, BUT, BABY,
YOU'VE GOT IT ALL, MY BABY.
YOU'VE GOT IT ALL INSIDE OF YOU.

Through the twists and turns of your early life,
    you always came out strong.
And I know it wasn't always easy,
    sometimes I was wrong.
I can tell you now my prayers for you
    are that you find yourself whatever you do.

CHORUS

© 1990 Evie Thompson

SONG #26
Metamorphosis

When I was young and so afraid,
    the cat had my tongue and my dreams went away.
Every night I cried myself to sleep,
lookin' for the light of a distant memory.

Then when the morning came
    and the shadows disappeared,
I remember what you said to me
    as you wiped away my tears.

FROM AN UGLY DUCKLING TO A SWAN
    THERE'S A METAMORPHOSIS
    FROM A CATERPILLAR THAT CAN'T GO ON.
THERE'S A METAMORPHOSIS
    FROM A GIRL INTO A WOMAN,
    FROM A BOY INTO A MAN,
    WHEN FROGS TURN INTO PRINCES
    AND THE BEAST TAKES BEAUTY'S HAND.
THERE'S A METAMORPHOSIS, METAMORPHOSIS,
METAMORPHOSIS.

Lost in the dark, I struggled to be free,
    tryin' to make my mark and fulfill my destiny.
Thru quakes and fires I trembled all alone,
    started to get tired of finding' my way home.

Then when the earth stood still
    and peace broke out again,
You took me to the top of a hill and said,
"You can fly, my friend."

CHORUS

Now sometimes on the brink of change,
    my heart starts cryin' loudly.
I wanna crawl back into my cage,
    but I keep on, but I keep on walkin' proudly.

CHORUS

SONG #27
Wings of Change

Goin' thru a midlife crisis wonderin' who I am,
    chuckin' my vices and flying 'round the land.
With the past behind me and the future out ahead,
    don't know what I'll be but I'm goin' where I'm
    led.

My skin's too tight, I don't fit anymore.
I don't know if I'm right, but I gotta see more, so I'm

FLYIN' ON THE WINGS OF CHANGE,
    GETTING' HIGH ON THE WINGS OF
    CHANGE.
DOIN' THINGS I NEVER DREAMED I COULD,
    EVERYTHING I SAID I WOULD.
I'M FLYIN' ON THE WINGS OF CHANGE.

Here today and gone tomorrow,
    packin' my bag.
Sayin' goodbye to sorrow,
    to whatever is a drag.
My mind is expanding,
    my heart is awake.
I'm takin' off and landin'
    in a whole new place.

EVIE THOMPSON (EVIE T.)

I can't hold back,
    can't pretend anymore.
My container's gonna crack,
    'cause I gotta be more.

CHORUS

Some people'd like to keep me on the ground,
    but I'm movin' like a bat out of hell.
I got my own radar, got my own way around.
The outside's always changing, but I know the pilot
    well.

CHORUS

SONG #28
All the Lights in Hollywood

When I moved down to Los Angeles,
     lookin' for a dream,
Thought I'd find some kind of starmaker's kiss,
     but things aren't what they seem.
Give me somethin' real, give me somethin' strong,
     take me anywhere they can hear my song, 'cause

I AM A STAR AND ALL THE LIGHTS IN
     HOLLYWOOD DON'T SHINE ANY BRIGHTER
     OR PROUDER THAN ME.
NO NEED TO GO FAR 'CAUSE ALL THE
     LIGHTS IN HOLLYWOOD CAN'T HOLD A
     CANDLE TO ME.

Walkin' down Sunset Boulevard thinkin'
     all that glitters is not gold.
A sea of pretty faces that were empty and cold
     and hidin' the fear of growin' old.
Give me someone who will lick the salt of my tears.
Give me someone who will honor all of my years,
     'cause

CHORUS

See--------------here I am.

143

EVIE THOMPSON (EVIE T.)

Free-------------catch me if you can-------------'cause

CHORUS

© 2000 Evie Thompson

SONG #29
Light Up the Stars

What if everything I did mattered?
    Would there be any great or small?
If I kept one child from being battered,
    would it make a difference for them all?
If I loved one man from the bottom of my soul,
    would I make my mark on the whole?
Would I

REACH INTO HEAVEN
    AND LIGHT UP THE STARS.
WOULD MY FLAME KEEP BURNIN'
    AND LIGHT UP THE STARS?

Does my life mean something beyond me,
    if I can't be Oprah or Princes Di?
Do the songs I sing go somewhere I can't see,
    to the ears of angels in the sky?
Does Creation's glory depend on me
    giving birth to my own mystery?
Would it

CHORUS

EVIE THOMPSON (EVIE T.)

Maybe all we do goes right into
    the universal future.
Was this God's plan
    when it began for us to

CHORUS

© 2001 Evie Thompson

SONG #30
Shadow Boxing

When I was young they told me
    the devil would get my soul.
So all my life I've been runnin'
    with Satan nippin' at my toes.
And then one day the bogeyman came callin', sayin'
    "Come out and fight with me."

SHADOW BOXING—
    THOSE FEELINGS DON'T BELONG
    TO ME (WHO SAID THAT?)
SHADOW BOXING—THE DEVIL MADE ME DO
    IT, CAN'T YOU SEE?
SHADOW BOXING—IT'S THEIR FAULT—
    THEY JUST DIDN'T GET CAUGHT.

Well, the bogeyman had me by the throat,
    had me pinned to the ground in a vise.
I figured my days were numbered,
    so I thought I'd start bein' nice.
But he took off his mask and I let out a scream,
    the bogeyman looked just like me

CHORUS

Now every night when I go to sleep
With me, myself and I,
    I go a round or two with old bogey.
And no matter how hard I try,
      I just can't shake him,
      can't seem to make him go away.

CHORUS

So I'll turn around, say hello, shake hands,
    'cause that ain't no devil, that's my shadow man.
Gotta quit that shadow boxing
    and start shadow dancing again.

SHADOW DANCING—
    WELL, I GUESS I DO FEEL LIKE
    THAT SOMETIMES.
SHADOW DANCING—
    MAYBE I AM RESPONSIBLE FOR MY
    OWN ACTIONS.
SHADOW DANCING—
    WELL, MAYBE I HAD SOMETHING
    TO DO WITH IT.

Shadow dancing, shadow boxing, shadow dancing, shadow boxing, etc.

SONG #31
Love Looking at Me

As I watched this baby born
    in the middle of a storm,
I heard his voice cry out,
    a new life in the crowd.
Another face, another generation.
    in this child I saw all creation.
And I asked myself, "Is this what it's all about?"
    Then he opened up his eyes and took away
    all my doubt.

AND I SAW LOVE LOOKIN' AT ME,
    WHERE I WAS BLIND I COULD SEE.
I SAW LOVE LOOKIN' AT ME,
    AND I KNEW I WAS FREE.
LOVE LOOKIN' AT ME.

As I held him in my arms
    wantin' to keep him from harm,
I saw my daughter smile,
    a woman now with a child.
Radiatin' with love's elarion,
    another star in our constellation.
And I knew he'd make it through,
    and I knew he'd grow up straight and tall.

Then he opened up his eyes and let me know
     he knew it all.

CHORUS

In the eyes of this child,
I caught a glimpse of the man.
A gentle spirit—oh, so wild,
     singin', "Catch me if you can."

CHORUS

SONG #32
Heartland

When a bomb goes off in Oklahoma City,
In America, land of the free;
And the winds of hate blow cold across the prairies
    and children die needlessly;
It is time (it is time) to stand up for love,
don't let the fear drag us down.
It's gotta stop (it's gotta stop), it's gone far enough.
    there ain't much time to turn it around.
We gotta go back to the

HEARTLAND INSIDE OUR SOULS,
    'CAUSE ALL THE REVENGE IS TAKIN'
    ITS TOLL.
HEARTLAND, WHERE WE CAN MEET.
HEARTLAND, IT'S A TWO-WAY STREET.
WE GOTTA LAY DOWN OUR ARMS
    AND HOLD OUT OUR HANDS
IN HEARTLAND.

Don't let the actions of a few bow us down in terror
    or tempt us to forsake humanity.
An eye for an eye means lookin' in the mirror
    and grantin' each other liberty.
It is time (it is time) to stand up for peace.
Let the walls come tumblin' down.

We gotta live (we gotta live) in harmony
　　or somethin's gonna turn it around.

CHORUS

Come--------------come live in Heartland
One----------------one people in Heartland
Now--------------we gotta go back to the

CHORUS

© 1995 Evie Thompson

SONG #33
Fascist Swing

Well, lay down your freedom and put on your boots.
　　March in a line to the beat of the group.
Follow like a lemming in the party parade.
　　Simulated people got it made in the shade.
Keep your opinions to yourself.
　　Take the military down off the shelf.
And do the fascist swing—it's the latest thing.

LET'S DO THE FASCIST SWING.
　　DANCE ON OUT TO THE RIGHT.
DO THE FASCIST SWING.
　　MAKE SURE THEM BLACK SHIRTS AIN'T
　　TOO TIGHT.
GET RID OF THEM FREE RADICALS
IN OUR SYSTEM.
　　THE LEFT SIDE'S ON SABBATICAL.
I'VE KINDA MISSED 'EM.
　　LET'S DO THE FASCIST SWING--
IT'S THE LATEST THING.

Control everyone and everything in sight
　　And don't talk back, it is not polite.
Take your orders from the top.
　　Watch out for ERA, it's a communist plot.

You're not really an individual,
>   It's much more fun to be anti-liberal.
So do the fascist—
>   It's the latest thing.

CHORUS

Rise up nation states and assume your position.
>   You gotta be on top of the opposition.
You better start a war 'cause the economy's down.
>   The buck's bein' passed, goin' 'round and 'round.
Forcible suppression—that's the style.
>   Well, grab yourself a partner for a while.
And do the fascist swing—
>   It's the latest thing.

CHORUS

© 1995 Evie Thompson

SONG #34
Dancing on the Wind

Through the years you walked by my side,
    through the tears you were my guiding light.
Every morning and every night,
    I knew I could count on you to make it all right.

And it's so hard to let you go now,
    but I know I gotta do it anyhow.
Goodbye my friend—we'll meet again.
    Farewell old friend, I'll see you when

WE'LL BE DANCING ON THE WIND
    LAUGHING AT THE RAIN,
    AND TELLIN' EVERYBODY THAT THERE
    AIN'T NO PAIN.
PLAYING IN THE FIELDS OF THE LORD OF
    CREATION,
    WRAPPED IN A BLANKET OF HIS
    ADORATION.
DANCING ON THE WIND,
    FLOATIN' ON CLOUDS
    THAT DISAPPEAR LIKE MISTS BEFORE THE
    SUN.
DANCING ON THE WIND,
    TOGETHER WE'LL GO HOME AGAIN,
    AND BRING BACK ALL THE LOVE THAT
    WE'VE BECOME.

EVIE THOMPSON (EVIE T.)

You taught me love with no condition,
Helped me find faith to hold to my vision.

You were an angel in disguise,
    my constant companion for every sunrise.
And I couldn't find the words to say,
    as I held you while you slipped away.
Goodbye my friend, we'll meet again.
    Farewell old friend, I'll see you when

CHORUS

Let me know when the dark is all around me.
    I can hear your heartbeat in the whispers of
    the moon.
Whoa——give me something to believe.
    I'm waiting for you, loving you and soon

CHORUS

SONG #35
Hurry Home

From the day you came into my life,
  no matter what you did,
  you healed my heart and soul.
Through the years in spite of all your fears,
  Right up until the end
  You helped to make me whole.
And lovin' you was all I could do, so

HURRY HOME NOW.
  TAKE MY LOVE, LEAVE THE PAIN.
HURRY HOME NOW
  AND CATCH THAT FREEDOM TRAIN.

I recall so many sweet hellos.
The feel of angels' wings
  when you lay next to me.
And I know I was so lucky to
  be there when you said goodbye—
  even through my agony—
All I could do was keep lovin' you, so

CHORUS

And when the wind blows
Send me a sign and

CHORUS

© 2000 Evie Thompson

SONG #36
Fly Away

Once upon a time, you were my best friend.
    A veteran of the same war, sisters 'til the end.
You were there when I was scared, and
    You were there for all the history we shared.
You were there but now you must dare
    to go your own way.

FLY AWAY, FLY AWAY SOFTLY.
    SURRENDER TO THE LIGHT.
FLY AWAY, FLY AWAY GENTLY.
    TO WHERE THERE IS NO NIGHT.
FLY AWAY HOME. FLY AWAY HOME.

When you close your eyes on this world at last,
    and open them on heaven, forget our
    troubled past.
And on and on, only the love goes on and on.
And when the music starts playin' on and on,
    remember me then and go on and on.

CHORUS

Help me find the strength to carry on.
    Soothe me with the wings of Halcyon.

And when angels come to be with you,
    remember...I will, too—

CHORUS

SONG #37
Arms Around America

We see her wounds,
> we hear her cries,
> we feel the terror in her skies.

The loss of lives
> and innocence,
> in the name of God, it makes no sense.

Will our children carry on this nation's sorrow?
> Could we be a clarion for a new tomorrow?

If we gave it our all and reached our

ARMS AROUND AMERICA,
> WEAVE A CHAIN OF MANY HANDS.

WITH OUR ARMS AROUND AMERICA,
> WE'LL SING FOR ALL SHE STANDS.

WITH OUR ARMS AROUND, ARMS AROUND
> AMERICA, AROUND AMERICA.

May hearts of stone melt from our tears,
> if we give into all our fears.

Then we have lost what makes us great,
> in the name of God, we cannot hate.

Only love will save us now.

From our own choices,
> only we can turn around—

Listen to the voices
> of the prophets of Peace and reach our

CHORUS

We are still free
    And we will rise above this inhumanity
And reach our

CHORUS

SONG #38
Mary, Tell Me

Mary, tell me, when did woman lose her place
    in His—Story?
And Mary, tell me, have I got this straight?
    'cause of one chromosome,
I don't get no glory? Whoa—
Mary, tell me, will I go to heaven
    if I didn't get pregnant by the Holy Ghost?
And, Mary, tell me, if I don't obey my husband
    will lightnin' turn me into toast? Whoa—

MARY, TELL ME, IF I EAT AN APPLE
    WILL THE MEN AROUND ME DROP LIKE
    FLIES?
O MARY, MARY,
    MAYBE I SHOULD HAVE BEEN
    ONE OF THE GUYS.

Mary, tell me, do I need a priest
    to turn me on to electricity?
And Mary, tell me, am I all washed up
    'cause my plumbin' went with my domesticity?
Whoa—
Mary, tell me, should I cover my body
    'cause my name is Eve and I'm a temptation?

Mary, tell me, if they throw me over when I rock the
boat, have I got flotation?

CHORUS

And I know I can be anything I want,
this is America after all.
I think I'll be a Pope.

CHORUS

© 2002 Evie Thompson

SONG #39
Life Moves On

From where I stand, a little older.
    A little further down the road.
I see your hands, you are the holders
    Of a future of your own.

I'm prayin' for your lives
    to be filled with laughter, comfort for your tears.
When your children come to me.
    I will hold them close and know that both of you
    are near.

LIFE MOVES ON,
    THE TIME HAS COME.
    WE'RE GONNA BE FREE.
LIFE MOVES ON,
    LOVE IS STRONGER
    THAN LEGACY.
LIFE MOVES ON, AND ON, AND ON, AND ON.

I watch you walk down that aisle
    and the tears are startin' to flow.
I hear you talk as you walk that mile,
    and I know I gotta let go.

I know you need to spread your wings
    and I'm so proud.
I hold you both so dear.
    If I could give you anything, I would give you
    love and let you know that I'll be here.

CHORUS

Make every moment count,
    don't let your past drag you down.
Treat each other like a gift,
    'cause it all passes by so quick.

CHORUS

© 1993 Evie Thompson

SONG #40
Dear Mr. Bush

I'm a child of the tsunami,
    I am living in the streets.
And my family is missing,
    Probly taken by the sea.
I have nowhere to go now,
    might be sold into slavery.
I cannot see my future,
    I might not live anyhow.

DEAR MR. BUSH, WHAT WOULD JESUS SAY?
    BILLIONS FOR WAR, BUT I HAVE NO
    FOOD TODAY.
DEAR MR. BUSH, I'M ONLY ONE OF
    MILLIONS.
OH, CAN'T YOU HEAR OUR VOICES
    ABOVE THE SOUND OF YOUR GUNS?

All that's left of my village
    is a pile of stones.
So many people dyin',
    so many children all alone.
And while we all have great spirit,
    there's just so much we can do.
The fate of my people
    is partly up to you.

CHORUS

P.S. Do I have to be a Christian
    for you to save the children?
Do your armies know the difference
    between mercy and war?

CHORUS

SONG #41
I'll Be There

The time has come when I must say goodbye.
    You're gonna be all right without me.
And when I get to heaven, I'll send you a sign,
    so you will know that you set me free.
I will never forget the touch of your hand
    or the lovin' in your eyes.
Have no regrets—
    an angel never dies.

I'LL BE THERE IN EVERY MELODY,
    IN EVERY SONG YOU SING.
I WILL LIVE AGAIN,
    I WILL DANCE AROUND YOU
    IN THE WIND.
AND WHEN IT RAINS,
    YOU CAN FEEL MY LOVE
    IN EVERY DROP OF RAIN.
I'LL BE THERE. I'LL BE THERE.

All those you loved will come to welcome me.
I'm gonna be all right, I'll be home.
But when I hear you callin', I'll come joyfully
    so you will know you are never alone.
If you listen real close, you'll hear the sweet sound
    of angels passing by.

A whisper of peace and comfort when you cry.

CHORUS

Hold me close inside your memory.
Celebrate all the years and love that you gave me.

CHORUS

© 2005 Evie Thompson

SONG #42
I'm Gonna Go Out Singin'

It used to seem so long,
    but it could all be over.
In a moment even the strong
    could be pushin' up clover--like that (snap!)
Don't always know what I've got
    until I start to lose it.
Life keeps puttin' me on the spot
    until I finally choose it.

I'M GONNA GO OUT SINGIN',
I'M GONNA GO OUT SINGIN'.
WHEN THEY SCATTER MY ASHES
    I'LL SING ON THE WIND.
WHEN LIGHTNIN' FLASHES
    MY SONG WILL BEGIN.
I'M GONNA GO OUT,
I'M GONNA GO OUT,
I'M GONNA GO OUT SINGIN'.

I used to just assume
    that there would be tomorrow.
Kept my heart inside a tomb
    with so much sorrow, and then (ha!)
I felt a belly laugh
    and a song start risin'.

I'll be dancin' to my epitaph
    out to the far horizon.

CHORUS

And I'll go on forever
    in the music of the air.
And you will always find me
    'cause I'll be everywhere.

CHORUS

© 2001 Evie Thompson

SONG #43
Riches to Rags (and Back Again)

I was born with a silver spoon,
    Cadillacs in the yard,
With cooks, maids, my very own room,
    doesn't sound too hard.
I traveled to Paris, stayed at the Ritz,
    played croquet in Biarritz.
I had diamonds, furs and Persian rugs.
    Woulda traded it all for hugs. I went from

RICHES TO RAGS
    AND BACK AGAIN.
EVEN ALL THE KING'S HORSES
    AND ALL THE KING'S MEN
COULDN'T GET THIS GENTLE HEART
    TO MEND.
I WENT FROM RICHES TO RAGS
    AND BACK AGAIN.
RICHES TO RAGS AND BACK AGAIN.

It wasn't 'til I lost my estate
    and life had taken its toll,
That I found this urge to create
    the music of my soul.
Don't have fame or fortune
    but I got me—

somethin' more than pedigree.
I got angels and love and the mystery
of worlds inside of me. I went from

CHORUS

Is this incarnation
the only one I've known?
I hope it's just another note
in a symphony of love
to bring me home.

CHORUS

SONG #44
For All the Women

I've never been cast upon a
    witch's funeral pyre, but
I've been burned by misogyny
    and silenced by hell-fire.
I know what it's like
    to fear for my life,
    in the haven of my own home.
And I can reach across the years
    and feel my sister's tears
    in another place and time.

AND SO I'LL SING FOR ALL THE WOMEN
    WHO'VE BEEN SILENCED FOR THEIR
    VIEWS.
I'LL DANCE FOR ALL THE WOMEN
    WHOSE FEET HAVE EVER BEEN BOUND.
YES, I'M GONNA MAKE LOVE
    FOR ALL THE WOMEN WHO'VE BEEN
    TAKEN OR ABUSED.
REMEMBER FOR ALL THE WOMEN
    THAT WE STAND ON COMMON GROUND.

I've never felt the guillotine
    or had to wear a veil.
But I've been chopped off at the knees

my soul's been put in jail.
I know what it's like to feel less-than
and be invisible.

Have we really come so far
when we're still judged for who we are,
like our sisters long ago?

CHORUS

We can hold hands
with our sisters everywhere.
And we can draw strength
if we know that they are there.

CHORUS

© 2002 Evie Thompson